YOU WOULDN'T BELIEVE!

44 STRANGE & WONDROUS DELMARVA TALES

Also by Jim Duffy/Secrets of the Eastern Shore:

• *Eastern Shore Road Trips:*
27 One-Day Adventures on Delmarva

• *Tubman Travels:*
32 Underground Railroad Journeys on Delmarva

• *Eastern Shore Road Trips #2:*
26 MORE One-Day Adventures on Delmarva

Website
SecretsoftheEasternShore.com

Bookstores, retail shops, and other purchase options
SecretsoftheEasternShore.com/product-category/books

Facebook
Facebook.com/SecretsoftheEasternShore

Feedback
SecretsoftheEasternShore@gmail.com
443.477.4490

YOU WOULDN'T BELIEVE!

44 STRANGE & WONDROUS DELMARVA TALES

A Secrets of the Eastern Shore Book
By Jim Duffy

You Wouldn't Believe!

Published by Secrets of the Eastern Shore
Cambridge, Maryland

Cover Design: Jill Jasuta
Interior Design: Paul Clipper
Proofreading & Research: Makena Duffy

ISBN: 978-1-7356741-3-1

Feedback
SecretsoftheEasternShore@gmail.com
443.477.4490

More Stories
SecretsoftheEasternShore.com

TABLE OF CONTENTS

You Wouldn't Believe!

INTRODUCTION

If you ever go looking for expert advice on writing a nonfiction book, this tip will land at the top of your priority list: Develop a strong theme. What one clear message do you want to send? What single thread ties everything together?

I gave these questions long, diligent consideration when it came time to write this introduction. Here is what I came up with: "LOOK! A SQUIRREL!"

I exaggerate. But not by much: Most stories in this book landed in my lap by accident or happenstance. I am a wanderer by nature. I'm a writer by trade. I grew into a history buff as years piled up. I came to write two books of *Eastern Shore Road Trips* that serve up a mix of travel advice and fun stories from days gone by.

I don't remember which Road Trips story I was researching on the day I jumped down the Gilbert Lare rabbit hole. I set out to find newspaper articles from the 1930s. My wandering eye darted across the page: Shore's Champion Jailbreaker Is Foiled at Federalsburg

The next four hours passed in the blink of an eye as I tracked the antics of a brash young antihero with Houdini-like skills—the "Del-Mar-Va Bandit," everyone called him. And so it goes with story after story in this book. I'd go looking for one thing and find another.

You Wouldn't Believe!

Life works like that sometimes.

Off you go, then—on this random excursion through strange & wondrous tales from the Delmarva Peninsula. Along the way there will be love stories and crime stories and funny stories and unbelievable stories and sad stories. Those flying mayonnaise jars are in here, too. Enjoy!

—Jim Duffy

You Wouldn't Believe!

CRITTERS!

JAKE THE ALLIGATOR

Paging through a book of photos from times gone by in Worcester County, Md., I came across a crazy postcard. The legend sketched out in a brief caption piles one ridiculous notion atop another. Wait, a man put an infant alligator in the mail? The alligator survived its postal journey? And ended up as a sort of civic mascot, shown off daily in a downtown Berlin storefront to the delight of shoppers?

Yup, it's all true.

Jake's Beginnings: A Cigar Box Journey

After some hunting around, I managed to find a couple of old newspaper stories that confirm this story in sketchy fashion. In 1872, Mr. Henry Godfrey of New York dropped an itty bitty baby alligator—seven adorable inches long—into a cigar box and mailed him to a friend in Berlin, which is a few miles inland from Ocean City. The box involved might have been a shoebox, not a cigar box. There are conflicting reports on this detail.

Dr. Henry C. Hudson immediately set about raising the critter. He christened his new pet "Jake." When Jake got big enough, Hudson put him on display in the shop window of his downtown drug store. When Hudson sold that drugstore to Dr. Thomas Y. Franklin, Jake was part of the deal. He stayed right there in the window.

In 2000, an enterprising reporter for the *Salisbury Daily Times* found a then-95-year-old woman named Doris Taylor who had fond memories of gawking at Jake through that storefront window:

He was the talk of the town. People came here [from other towns] just to see "that alligator."

Eventually, Jake outgrew the window. By 1906, he measured six feet, four inches long and weighed 125 pounds. He was moved into Dr. Franklin's backyard, which is where he must have been relaxing while modeling for that strange old picture postcard, considering the chicken wire and wagon wheels visible in the background.

A Farewell to Jake
Jake died in 1909. But before we get to his obituary, here are a few extraneous facts I picked up from those old newspaper articles:

• An unnerving quote from one article: Jake "has escaped several times, but has been re-captured without much difficulty."

• Jake ate raw meat, any kind of raw meat. He wasn't picky. He could down five pounds on a ravenous summer day.

• During colder months, Jake ate nothing. From October into June, he would lie in a "comatose" state, waking only once he was 100 percent sure that the weather was more to his liking. I have a few winter-dreading acquaintances who are going to be jealous of Jake when they read this.

• Parents in Berlin used to invoke Jake's name when angry with unruly children. As in, "If you don't stop misbehaving this instant, I will feed you to Jake!"

• In the summer of 1905, Jake was packed up into some sort of vehicle and transported to Ocean City, where he went on display in carnival side show fashion.

Jake didn't get the full obituary treatment. Instead, the *Democratic Messenger* newspaper of nearby Snow Hill reported his passing in a column devoted to society happenings. Word of Jake's demise is sandwiched in between a report about a Women's Auxiliary meeting at St. Paul's Episcopal and a guest Sunday school speaker at Buckingham Presbyterian.

• Here is the memorial paragraph:

Jake Alligator, for 35 years a resident of Berlin, died last week, was skinned, and will reappear in his old place, Dr. Franklin's drug store, in the near future [after a taxidermist completes his work]. [Jake] has been an object of interest in the town through the years.

Rest in peace, Jake.

Postscript: Mystery of the Afterlife

Sometime in the years that followed, Jake went missing. No one seems to know what happened to his taxidermied body. Could Jake still be out there, hibernating and forgotten up in an attic or out in a barn or garage?

Speaking as an author, it would be great if this book sold a gazillion copies. But it might be even greater if this story found its way to Jake's current owner and inspired him or her that it's high time Jake made a triumphant return. That dead alligator belongs on a pedestal somewhere in downtown Berlin, don't you think?

Sika Snippets: Shinto Gods, Sexual Prowess, Ray Lewis

Rich guys do crazy things with money sometimes. Consider the case of Clement Henry. Born during the Civil War into a prominent Eastern Shore family, he grew up to become an itinerant businessman whose dealings stretched from a big department store in Chattanooga, Tenn. to an importing business in New York City that specialized in lace.

He made lots of money, and he had fun spending it. Sometime around 1916 he got a hankering to dip into the exotic-animal market. He bought a handful of "Japanese" deer from a European dealer. The details on this purchase are pretty thin. Some reports put the initial deer count at four, others at six.

Either way, this is how the Delmarva Peninsula came to be home today to between 10,000 and 15,000 those foreign sika deer. In trying to track this sika saga, I ended up jumping down some unexpected rabbit holes. Think legends about Shinto gods in Japan, aphrodisiac folk remedies in China, the near extinction of the great blue heron, and a strange interlude involving Pro Football Hall of Famer Ray Lewis.

Disappearing Ducks and Deer

At first, Henry seems to have locked his Japanese deer up in a pen at his home near the Dorchester County town of Cambridge, Md.

Why did he want Japanese deer? The cute factor is one possibility. Sika are smaller than our native whitetails, with a run of adorable white spots along the spine. Lots of folks have described them as looking like children's toys, especially when young. Perhaps Henry got them as an over-the-top gift for grand-kids? Or perhaps they seemed the perfect finishing touch on a Japanese garden—those too were in vogue among some circles at that time.

More likely, they were part of a grander plan. The early 1900s were a worrisome time for nature-loving outdoorsmen like Henry. The one-two punch of habitat loss and over-harvesting had nearly wiped out the population of native whitetail deer. Water-fowl populations were shrinking too, thanks in no small part to the practice of indiscriminate "market" hunting that had gunmen wielding cannon-like firearms and killing hundreds of birds at a time, which they then sold to hungry big-city markets.

Not all hunters went in for this mass mayhem. Sportsmen of a more traditional bent were as horrified by shrinking wildlife populations as anyone. They joined with various other groups of nature lovers in a push for wildlife protection. The Migratory Bird Act of 1918 outlawed market gunning for waterfowl and limited hunting activity to certain "seasons." The act is often credited with saving the great blue heron from extinction. Maryland made big moves in this time frame to limit deer hunting too, with an eye especially on protecting female does.

Rich guys like Henry took action on their own. They started buying up islands in the Chesapeake Bay with plans to transform them into private wildlife refuges where they and their friends could still go hunting, presumably in more sustainable ways.

That's why Albanus Phillips, a co-owner of the fabulously successful Phillips Packing Company of Cambridge, bought Bloodsworth Island in 1921. He was not alone, as the *Wilmington (Del.) Morning News* made clear while reporting on this development on Sept. 22, 1921:

Dorchester County is fast becoming a favorite place for the purchase of lands for game preserves. T. Coleman DuPont owns the Moors in [the] Neck district and [a] large tract in Hurley's Neck, Drawbridge district. Alfred I. DuPont has Cherry Island, off Morris Neck [on the] Little Choptank River; Charles H. Ford of St. Louis recently bought Ragged Point as a sporting place and game preserve. Clement Henry purchased James Island for the same purpose.

Located near Taylors Island at the mouth of the Little Choptank, James Island is nearly drowned today. But when Europeans first settled in those parts in the 1600s, it stretched across 1,300 acres. Twenty families were still living out there in the 1890s, but the place was shrinking badly and erosion would soon drive everyone to the mainland.

By the time Clement Henry bought the place, it was uninhabited and down to 185 acres. After making that purchase, he moved his Japanese deer out to the island.

The China Connection. Oh, and Ray Lewis

Technically speaking, sikas aren't deer at all. They belong to the elk family. Big sika populations once roamed all over East Asia, but that region endured its own version of the story of habitat loss and excessive hunting. The creatures are few and far between today in places like China, Korea, and Vietnam that once had them in abundance.

The Chinese call sika the "plum blossom deer." Folk medicine traditions there regard scrapings taken from the antlers of young sika as an aphrodisiac and all-around health booster. That notion is still in vogue today, as you can see for yourself by searching the internet for the dietary supplement called "deer antler velvet."

The aphrodisiac angle here is probably related to the fact that while male sika spend much of the year wandering solo through the landscape, they become shameless, sex-mad lotharios during the early autumn mating season, assembling temporary "harems" that can number up to a dozen ladies.

Deer antler velvet has also come into play in recent years as a sports supplement. Hall of Fame linebacker Ray Lewis of the Baltimore Ravens was involved in a supremely weird controversy in 2013 over allegations that he'd been shopping for the stuff while trying to rush back onto the field after a serious triceps injury.

Lewis denied ever using deer antler dust—it's banned by the NFL—and he was never found guilty of the offense. But that didn't stop the publicity about his case from sending sales of the supplement into the stratosphere. Two days after the news of the Lewis allegations broke, one deer antler velvet dealer reported that sales had increased by a factor of eight. Another reported "the biggest sales days ... since we launched."

Making Themselves at Home

Clement Henry's sika ran wild out on James Island. Adapting quickly to life in a mix of marsh and forest, his Japanese deer population reached an estimated 270 by the mid-1950s. That number dropped to 100 after a forest fire caused a foliage shortage that led to mass starvation in the winter of 1957. But the population soon rebounded.

Meanwhile, the deer had started to appear on Taylors Island by the 1930s. That development is hardly a surprise, as the animals are strong swimmers and Taylors is quite nearby. And so the slow march began. Researchers in the 1960s reported that sika had spread to about one-third of the Dorchester County mainland. Today, they roam all of Dorchester and have crossed into parts of Wicomico and Somerset counties.

The sika population on Assateague Island in Worcester County, Md. and Accomack County, Va. has a different backstory. They are descended from a few sikas that Clement Henry gifted or sold to a physician in Berlin, Dr. Charles Law. Law, in turn, sold a dozen deer to a local Boy Scout troop whose adult leader was likely Daniel Trimper of the family that ran Trimper's Resort in Ocean City, Md.

That resort is where the scouts put the deer on display as a tourist attraction, presumably as some sort of fundraising gimmick. The novelty of that show wore off after a little while, and the scouts eventually decided to free their deer on Assateague Island.

As the numbers of both these sika populations rose, hunters took notice. Sika hunts were happening on Taylors Island as early as 1938, but the outdoorsmen crowd didn't start showing up in really big numbers until the 1960s and 1970s. State wildlife regulators encouraged this trend by setting super high harvest numbers, as they were worried that the "invasive" sika would hinder efforts to rebuild the population of native whitetails.

That fear turned out to be mostly misplaced. Delmarva's sikas prefer to live on low-lying lands that the whitetail don't much like. The trick going forward in wildlife management will be to maintain that balance by keeping sika numbers at a level where they don't invade whitetail turf. The modern-day hunting limits are also set with an eye toward reaching a just-right population that's high enough to support the economic benefits of a hunting industry but low enough to limit the amount of crop damage suffered by farmers.

Among hunters, sika have a cool nickname—the "marsh ghost." The animals are largely nocturnal. With eyes set wide apart, they have fabulous peripheral vision. They tend to hang out in the deepest, most inaccessible stretches of marshland. This makes for a very challenging hunting experience, which is why the number of knowledgeable local guides offering their services for hire now runs into the hundreds.

Another sika snippet: When mosquitoes in the marsh get too oppressive, sikas head into so-called mud "wallows," basically burying themselves in soupy marsh muck in the way little kids might "bury" each other in the sand at Ocean City.

Turning Japanese
Current estimates place the sika population on Delmarva at between 10,000 and 15,000. That probably ranks as the second-largest in the world. The largest population is in Japan, which is where you should go if you grow tired of searching locally for these elusive "ghosts."

One place where they are easy to find is Nara Park in the Japanese city of that name—it's just west of Osaka. Some 1,200 wild sika wander the 1,240 acres of that park. Visitors are encouraged to buy Shika-senbei (nutritious deer crackers) and feed the elks. Sometimes, sikas appear to ask for food in a gesture that looks like a formal bow. Search the web for "bowing deer of Nara, Japan" and you'll see adorable videos of how this works.

You Wouldn't Believe!

Two pieces of advice if you go to Nara. First, don't bring your gun. Sika have been protected since ancient times in this park, which occupies a holy site dotted with temples. Legend has it that a Shinto god named Takemikazuchi-no-mikoto once visited the park site while riding a divine white deer. Because of that legend, killing sika at Nara ranked for centuries as a crime punishable by death. That penalty is off the table nowadays, but a recent case involving a crossbow hunter ended with a sentence of six months in jail.

Second piece of advice: Don't treat the Nara deer like pets. More than 100 park visitors a year suffer minor injuries trying to have a little fun while feeding deer. The Nara Park powers that be have now erected signs in English, Chinese, and Japanese reminding tourists that the deer are wild animals and begging visitors not to tease or toy with them while doling out crackers.

Postscript: Of Burials and Linguistics
In 2017, archeologists working the 5,000-year-old Guangfulin Ruins near Shanghai, China reported new sika-related discoveries. Only the most ornate gravesites there, it seems, contain pottery adorned with the twin images of sika deer and tomahawk-like weapons. Chinese families at that time often sacrificed an animal and buried it with their loved ones. Usually, it was a pig. But in the graves of the filthy rich—you guessed it, they were buried with sika companions.

The researchers interpreted these findings to mean that sikas served in Chinese lore as powerful symbols of wealth and power. To back up their theory, they pointed out that the ancient Chinese characters for sika deer formed a soundalike homonym with the words that mean "fat salary." It seems, then, that Clement Henry's interest in these exotic-to-him creatures wasn't all

You Wouldn't Believe!

that new—rich guys have been obsessing over sika deer across five millennia.

An Aerial Assault on Hog Island Light

The scene that unfolded on a late-winter night in 1900 on Hog Island was straight out of the Alfred Hitchcock classic The Birds. A flurry of unusual avian activity was in the air along the Atlantic Flyway that February, thanks to a long, unseasonable stretch of warm weather that fooled bevies of birds into starting their northbound spring migrations earlier than usual.

A barrier island off the oceanside of Virginia's Eastern Shore, Hog Island sits right along that flyway. The lighthouse there was an 1893 beacon built in a style known as "pile design," with nine iron legs splayed around a central cylinder. Birds often have trouble around lighthouses, as blinking beacons in the dead of night can leave them disoriented.

Here, for example, is a description of that odd behavior written by George Sterling, whose term as assistant keeper on Hog Island came a few years after the 1900 incident at the heart of this story.

The birds insensibly head for the light, and as the lantern turns on a pivot and flashes every forty-five seconds, the extreme glare blinds and bewilders them, and they strike with such force against the reflector that sometimes every bone in their body is smashed.

A Bevy of Brants Lose Their Minds

By the time Sterling arrived at Hog Island, the light atop that 190-foot-tall tower had been encased in thick wire netting. This was done in the aftermath of the avian assault that unfolded on Feb. 22, 1900.

From the book, *The Lightkeepers' Menagerie: Stories of Animals at Lighthouses:*

A frenzy, the cause of which was unknown, broke out. Birds began to fly at the lighthouse and slam the walls and lantern. They came with such force the keepers thought they were bent on destroying the lighthouse. Repeatedly, in waves, they bombed the lantern like kamikazes, shattering the glass windows and striking the expensive prism lens.

Keeper George Doughty and an assistant sprinted up the stairs to the top of the lighthouse, where they commenced trying to shoo away the invaders with waving arms and loud noises, thinking this would do the trick. They were wrong.

All-out war erupted. Shouts and banged pans soon gave way to clubs and sticks. Then, shots were fired in the air. When this failed to repel the feathered raiders, the guns were turned on the birds.

The two keepers ran out of ammunition. They gave up the fight after that, taking cover in a protected alcove below the lantern. When they emerged at dawn, bird carcasses covered the catwalk around the lighthouse tower. Below that, on the ground, bird bodies "littered the earth like confetti." Many of the poor things were still twitching in agony.

The keepers dug a trench and tossed the birds into a mass grave. Amazingly, the light was still shining. I have come across conflicting reports about whether the follow-up assault happened the very next night, or a couple of days later. The keepers did nothing this time around, and the birds retreated much more quickly than they had on the first assault. But the damage done in that second attack put Hog Island Light out of service for a stretch.

Fleeting Glimpses of Brantly Beauty

It's only fitting, I think, to take a moment here to pay tribute to those unfortunate birds. Most of the dead ones that night were American Brants. These small geese, with black heads and white necklaces, make annual migrations that are unusually long and arduous for their kind, running between the upper reaches of the Canadian Arctic and the southeastern U.S. coast.

In his 1908 book, *The Huntsman in the South*, outdoorsman Hunter Alexander shares a different, but related memory from a night he spent staying at the lighthouse on Hog Island. A terrible storm was blowing when an assistant keeper rousted Alexander from his bed and told him to climb up into the tower. Most of the stairway they took was exposed to the stormy elements.

The full force of the raging wind, filled with sleet and snow, struck us with such force that we staggered like drunken men. Inch by inch we worked and battled our way until we reached the tower.

Safe inside that warm refuge, Alexander watched as brants circled the light in a state of utter confusion.

It was a sight worth taking a long journey to see. The brant, the shyest, wildest, most timid of waterfowl, were within

*five feet of us, but, evidently blinded by the light, they could see
nothing. Some would circle around the tower, others dart by;
and wonderful to relate, some would remain stationary in the air,
their wings moving so rapidly that they were blurred like a wheel
in rapid motion. I thought at the time what a tremendous power
must lie in their wings to enable them to nullify the wind ... blowing sixty-five miles an hour.*

    *What a treat to be able to gaze on those wild birds ...
when they were free and unfettered in their native element, two
hundred feet above the earth! The lamp in the tower revolved
every forty-five seconds, [so that every bird spent] a short time
in the vivid glare, which displayed every graceful curve of neck
and head, and the set and balance of the body, and enabled one to
look into their brilliant eyes.*

    *The brant is not a glossy, showy bird like the wood duck
or mallard, but in the driving rain and under the powerful rays
of the lamp they were exquisitely beautiful; their plumage looked
like ebony, and the tints changed to many an iridescent hue. It
was enthralling to watch them dart in the midst of the ... refulgent
gleams, one second vivid and tangible, the next swallowed up in
... darkness.*

    *After two hours spent in the tower I returned to bed, and
in my dreams I could still see the darting, circling brant. Nature
has richly endowed Hog Island. I question whether there is any
other one spot on earth where fish, flesh, and fowl are more abun-
dant.*

Postscript: Hog's Light, Across the Bay

The light that shone from Hog Island in those days was a classic—a massive First Order Fresnel Lens that stood 10 feet tall,
weighed 2,500 pounds, and had 368 unique prisms. Today, this

rare relic of the past has an estimated worth well over $1 million.

The lighthouse was demolished by dynamite in 1948, but that lens was saved and eventually given to the Mariners Museum in Newport News, Va. From there it went on loan to the western shore city of Portsmouth, where it landed in storage for many years but eventually ended up on display in that city's historic district.

A 2004 article in *Lighthouse Digest* recounts the meticulous efforts to repair and restore that lens for public display in a glass enclosure along the Portsmouth seawall. At the very end of the piece, the author makes mention of the bird attack in 1900. "This tale might account for some of the damage now visible in the lens. But against all odds, this striking work of art and technology has survived and will shine for many years to come."

The last of Hog Island's human residents fled for the mainland after a run of brutal hurricanes and floods in the 1930s. Modern-day brants don't have to worry about man-made hazards, as the island is now owned by the Nature Conservancy and managed as a bird sanctuary.

THE MAN WHO DESPISED HOG ISLAND

Through most of the Civil War, the Union Army had a significant presence on the Eastern Shore of Virginia—that stretch of the peninsula was effectively under federal occupation. This is how 20-year-old George W. Bonsall ended up on Hog Island in the thick of summertime, 1864.

He was a member of the 138th Regiment Ohio National Guard. He kept a diary, recounting how a place he and his fellow soldiers expected to be a "little paradise" became instead a "wretched island" that they were all desperate to leave. The villain of the piece will be familiar to all of us modern-day wanderers who have made summertime excursions into remote natural settings.

Saturday, July 30
We left Cherrystone about 7 o'clock. The distance to Hog Island is about forty miles. ... The boys were all delighted with the pleasant prospect before them. We all supposed Hog Island, notwithstanding its not very elegant name, was a little paradise, and we

*were informed that the people were all loyal [to the Union], and
we were prepared to enjoy ourselves, as much as these favorable
circumstances would admit.*

Arrived at our destination at 2.15 pm. ...

*The mosquitoes of this island are most horrid-looking
"animals"—they can hardly be termed "insects" on account of
their size and ferocity. They attack us in broad daylight. Had a
very good supper this evening—coffee, bread, & fried bacon.*

*After supper I went down to the beach. Remained there
for some time, watching the immense billows which roll one after
another upon the beach. Between the lighthouse and the ocean is
a broad, bare expanse of sandy beach, between one and two miles
wide.*

*The mosquitoes attacked us in force tonight. I covered my
head with my handkerchief and woolen blanket, but the "gallinippers" bit me [through] the blanket, and kept up such an uproari-
ous noise around my head that it was some time before I could get
to sleep.*

Sunday, July 31

*The boys tell some very large stories this morning concerning
the "skeeters," and some of [the boys] are [so] disfigured with
red, black, and blue marks, swollen eyes, and other marks of the
terrible charge, as to be scarcely recognizable. The gallinippers
show no mercy—they go in with demonic yells and inflict such
terrible punishment on their unhappy victims that the poor fel-
lows are hardly recoverable the next day.*

This is our "Paradise."!!

*... After breakfast with several others, I made a general
tour of observation through the island. It is seven miles long and
about two miles wide, including the beach.*

You Wouldn't Believe!

... There are on the island, I am informed, 60 persons, constituting ten families—simple, goodhearted, talkative people, as far as I have seen, & all very loyal [to the Union]. Not one of them voted for Secession except the then keeper of the lighthouse. ... The houses are very small, generally having but one or two rooms, and are constructed in primitive style but are kept very neat and clean. The men fish and follow the sea; the women are very industrious. But little land is under cultivation.

Found plenty of beach plums and wild cherries and some very good blackberries.

There is only one cart on the whole island. There is no road—the houses are all built along a narrow footpath which runs [through] the island.

I am informed by one of the "oldest inhabitants" that the proper name of this island is "Teach's Island," being named after a very cruel pirate chieftain of that name, whom the elderly inhabitant said had buried an immense amount of treasure some-where on the island, which has not yet been found.

This elderly gentleman said the island was once a pleas-ant, abiding place but the sand has "taken possession of it." Near the beach, the sand has been blown on the hills, covering them to a depth of many feet. The elderly inhabitant states that the limits of this island are constantly becoming smaller.

Nobody appears to know why the island is called "Hog Island," but it is supposed that an immense porker—the largest ever raised in the country—was raised here and the island was named in honor of this great event. Don't know whether this story is true or not, but ... there is now but very little livestock of any kind—a few sheep and cows but not half a dozen horses fit for use.

Returned to "Camp" at 12:30 o'clock. I can't imag-

ine why we were sent here. ... The people say there is no guard needed. The place has never been visited by guerrillas, and if it should be they would soon leave in disgust.

The people are very poor. We are tormented day and night by the mosquitoes. Fishhawks are the only game to be found. On the whole, I come to the conclusion that Hog Island would be a most excellent place to go away from!!

Monday, August 1
Lt. Timberman and several others ... went to Eastville Sunday morning in an open rowboat, and returned in the same manner. They went to request the Colonel to remove us from this wretched island.

Murray built a large fire near our tent last night after supper and the smoke from this kept the gallinippers away for a long time, but when the fuel was burnt up they attacked us. Many of the boys slept on the beach near the water's edge. They say the mosquitoes do not trouble them there.

Wednesday, August 3
Slept very well during the night, but early in the morning I was charged upon by an army of mosquitoes, who soon drove sleep from "mine eyes." I covered my head with my blanket and listened to the angry, demoniac yells & shrieks of rage and disappointment of the baffled fiends.

I think I have heard more "loud swearing" since we came to Hog Island than I ever heard in half a year before.

The boys are all in good spirits. We are going to leave this island.

Mr. Bonsall survived his wartime tour of duty, then returned to his hometown of Cincinnati, where he embarked on a career as a carpenter. While I can't say for sure one way or the other, it's probably safe to assume that he never returned to Hog Island.

THE FOXXY TERRIER WHO FOUND ITSELF

The dog-gone-missing report that came into the Dover, Del. police department in November of 1935 got lots of extra attention—and for good reason. The fox terrier in question belonged to Maryland native Jimmie Foxx.

Everyone on the Delmarva Peninsula knew that name in those days. Born in Sudlersville, Md., Foxx had slugged his way into baseball's major leagues in 1925, at the tender age of 17. From that moment on he'd been building a baseball resume for the ages, one that would eventually land him in the Baseball Hall of Fame.

The incident began when Foxx left his "prize-winning" fox terrier—what other breed would Jimmie Foxx have?—in the care of his father-in-law, Charles Heite. Heite lived across the border in Delaware, along the road between Marydel and Dover. You can probably imagine the panic Heite felt when that dog went missing, far from home and in surroundings that may have been quite unfamiliar.

Heite called the police for help. The cops jumped into action. In Dover, a description of the missing pooch was distributed to all officers, along with a head's up about its VIP owner. Alas, the police searches came up empty.

I will let the *Crisfield (Md.) Post* tell you what happened next:

Early Monday evening, Lt. Oliver and Officer Moore were working [at the] police headquarters [in Dover]. They heard a commotion in the hall and a dog walked into the room, sat on the floor, and proceeded to look over the officers. Lt. Oliver studied the dog and then called it by name, to which it gave an immediate response.

After proper entries were made in the case showing that the fugitive had surrendered, the dog was given a ride in the police car and returned to [Mr. Heite]. The dog, of course, failed to give an explanation for or account of its wanderings.

Postscript: Land of the Foxx

If you'd like to learn more about the Jimmie Foxx story without traveling to the Hall of Fame in upstate New York, head to his birthplace in Sudlersville. A statue of him stands in a small park at the center of town. Plus, the Sudlersville Train Station Museum has a fun collection of Foxx memorabilia. Be sure to check in advance—the museum is only pen occasionally. There is also an extended write-up about Foxx's fascinating life in an excursion devoted to baseball history in my second book of *Eastern Shore Road Trips.*

THIS CRAB CAN SAVE YOUR LIFE

To say that the horseshoe crab is an ancient creature would be an understatement. Classical Rome, that's ancient, at a couple of thousand years. Fossil experts guesstimate the age of the *Limulus polyphemus* at 450 million years. Horseshoe crabs were waddling around in dinosaur times.

In my first book of *Eastern Shore Road Trips*, I wrote a little bit about the natural wonder of the horseshoe-crab mating ritual that unfolds every spring on the shores of Delaware Bay. Horseshoes emerge from that salty water in astounding numbers, clambering up onto the sand under a romantic full or new moon. The fecundity of female horseshoes is astonishing. Over the course of a few sex-filled days, each one can lay between 80,000 and 100,000 eggs. Those eggs are packed with nutrition, which is why scads of hungry migrating shorebirds try to crash the party.

Horseshoes live up and down the Atlantic Coast, but the epicenter of the population is in our Delaware Bay. Thousands of nature lovers make pilgrimages to the beaches above Lewes every May and June to watch this astounding mating ritual. A couple of towns even hold festivals in honor of *Limulus polyphemus*.

But our prehistoric neighbor has another claim to fame—and it's one that has impacted your life and protected your health. Have you gotten a vaccine shot? Have you or a loved one had occasion to use a catheter, a pacemaker, or IV tube? How about contact lens fluid? Horseshoe crabs are blessed with a biological anomaly that modern scientists use to ensure the safety of these and countless other medications and medical devices.

Of Blue Blood and Primitive Laboratories
The story of how our horseshoe became a lifesaver begins in 1963 on Cape Cod, in a famous research facility called the Marine Biological Laboratory. That's where Jack Levin—then a young postgraduate "fellow" whose specialty of hematology involves disorders of the blood—had been sent by his bosses at Johns Hopkins in Baltimore.

I had the honor of meeting Levin while working up a more science-oriented version of this story for the alumni magazine of Johns Hopkins University. Much of the material here comes from that story.

When he arrived on Cape Cod, Levin knew next to nothing about the assignment at hand. He soon found himself following his new boss, the pathobiologist Frederik Bang, into a primitive-looking laboratory with a rudimentary "sea table" and a dingy aquarium tank. Inside that tank were some prehistoric-looking marine arthropods. When they moved, seawater splashed onto the floor.

"Pick one out," Bang said, pointing to the creatures.

Levin knew nothing of *Limulus polyphemus*. When he heard the words horseshoe crab, his mind jumped to blue crabs. He'd been in Maryland long enough to know about the damage blue crab pincers can do. He figured this new creature would be at least as dangerous—it had 10 claws set under a military-style helmet and backed by a long, malevolent-looking tail.

"I was scared to death," he says.

Bang was having fun with his newbie researcher. Despite appearances, horseshoe crabs are mostly harmless. Those 10 claws will grasp at you, but the result is more hug than bite. In another bit of playfulness, Bang didn't bother to tell Levin that a smidgeon of copper in Limulus' biological mix causes its blood to take on a strange, almost otherworldly shade of milky blue.

"If you're not expecting it, that's quite a sight," Levin laughs.

That blood is central to a tale of scientific innovation that has been a boon to human health. Together, Levin and Bang published a run of papers in the 1960s that examined the bacteria-fighting secrets of blue horseshoe blood. Using those blood cells, Levin then developed a test that ensures medications and medical devices have not been contaminated with dangerous bacteria.

That Limulus amebocyte lysate [LAL] test has saved millions of lives and prevented countless illnesses. It's used on drugs, intravenous fluids, vaccines, and all manner of medical devices. COVID-19 vaccines had to pass horseshoe-crab muster, too. All this started in a lab with no hot water or working air conditioning.

"The conditions Bang and Levin worked in were so austere," marvels Jim Cooper, a colleague of Levin's and a nuclear pharmacist who played his own role in developing the LAL test and turning it into a successful commercial product. "They had none of the lab equipment we take for granted now. They didn't have the computers we have. They didn't have software. To me, what they accomplished is all the more impressive because of that."

In Pursuit of Seemingly Aimless Science

Everyone has read stories about scientists wasting taxpayer dollars. A few years back, the headlines went to $3.4 million spent studying aggression and anxiety in male hamsters. Then there were the researchers who gave cocaine to honeybees. The list goes on and on.

Frederik Bang was doing that kind of research on horseshoe crabs. He had made notable discoveries about malaria, cystic fibrosis, and cancer during his distinguished career, but he had an oddball streak, too. A man of insatiable curiosity, he found his way to that blue blood because he was a big believer in studying the biology of marine creatures at a time when conventional wisdom—the "scientific consensus," in our modern parlance—held that research on animals was best conducted on mammals, our closest biological relatives.

Bang bucked that wisdom, arguing that "transparent" sea creatures held great potential for generating insights into the workings of human biology. During the summers of 1953 and 1954, Bang conducted a series of what he dubbed "naive experiments" with *Limulus polyphemus*. The coastal waters where horseshoe crabs live are chock-full of bacteria, and Bang was curious about which of the many pathogens in that water posed a threat to horseshoes. What sort of defenses had the creature had developed?

The work involved injecting crabs with various types of bacteria to identify which substances were toxic and at what levels. Bang was struck by the way *Limulus* blood clotted amid some bacterial invasions. He speculated that the clotting happened so as to trap pathogens inside biological bubbles that served like life-sentence jail cells, keeping infectious substances from spreading.

Bang stored bacterial samples from those tests in a freezer

at Woods Hole. Then he did ... nothing. Nearly a decade passed, until one day he asked the head of hematology at Johns Hopkins if he might be able to borrow the blood expertise of one of his young researchers.

No one seems to remember what sparked Bang's renewed interest in that blue blood. Did he stumble across those old samples in a freezer? Did he see something in the literature or on a sea table that brought those gloppy horseshoe-blood bubbles to mind?

In any case, Jack Levin won the assignment of helping Bang solve the hematological mysteries of this ancient sea creature.

"Bang quickly became a hero of mine," Levin said. "He had an incredible mix of curiosity, passion, and scientific instinct. How many researchers out there who are working at his level are going to drop everything to think the way he did about these horseshoe crabs? The answer is either 'Next to nobody' or 'Nobody.'"

More Sensitive Than Rabbit Butts
The COVID-19 pandemic is just a recent chapter in a story that runs through all of human history. Viruses and bacteria are the deadliest enemies of our species. Think smallpox—traces of that virus have been found in 3,000-year-old Egyptian mummies. It killed some 300 million people in the 1900s alone. The infamous Black Death was a bacterial plague that wiped out more than half of Europe's population in the 1300s.

Only in recent centuries have humans found effective ways to fight these enemies. The first vaccine appeared in the late 1700s. Modern syringes that made it safer and faster to administer vaccines showed up in the 1800s. But these tools opened the way for a bacterial counterattack—a mysterious, dangerous, and sometimes fatal "injection fever" that arose after patients received shots.

It wasn't until the 1920s that the culprit was identified as a class of bacteria scientists call "Gram negative endotoxins." The work of biochemist Florence Siebert led to the development of an early test for the presence of these endotoxins in medications. That test involved giving the substance to a panel of rabbits. If enough rabbits developed fevers, the substance was contaminated.

In its time, this "rabbit test" was a godsend, widely used by pharmaceutical companies and medical device makers. But it was also costly and cumbersome. Levin administered a few rabbit tests early in his career. It's an experience he hasn't forgotten, as the temperature measurements were taken by way of the butt.

"As one of the last people alive who's actually done this, I can tell you that it takes quite a bit of skill," he says with a wince. "Rabbits don't enjoy it very much when you stick things up their rectum, and the claws on their back feet can do a lot of damage."

By the 1960s, medical advances were pushing up against the limits of what the rabbit test could handle. In the field of nuclear medicine, for example, some newly developed medications had a shelf life measured in hours. It took at least a full day for the results from rabbit tests to come back.

Back to horseshoes. Levin came to his blue-blood project with no special interest or background in marine biology. His mission was to study the blood-coagulation mechanisms at work in *Limulus polyphemus*. That work immediately hit a roadblock. The blood samples Levin prepared began clotting in a matter of hours.

"They'd look fine when I left the lab, but the next morning was another story," he recalls. "You can't study blood cells in that condition—the blood needs to stay fluid."

He tried every anticoagulant trick in the book. Nothing worked. Levin had done some research on blood coagulation in rabbits, so he knew that bacterial endotoxins could kick that process into gear in at least one other species. What if things worked the same way in this marine arthropod as it did in that mammal?

The next time he drew horseshoe crab blood, he did so after making 1,000 percent sure that his glass tubes and other tools were free of such bacterial contamination. The blood didn't clot. Now he was off and running, with a new focus on the horseshoe crab's defenses against a very specific (and dangerous to humans) enemy, endotoxins.

The discoveries came fast and furious in the next few years. The key to the coagulation system lies with mobile blood cells called amebocytes that release proteins in response to the appearance of gram-negative endotoxins. Levin soon realized that the system is phenomenally sensitive, picking up the tiniest traces of contamination.

He then set out to transform these revelations into something useful. Soon, he was washing horseshoe amebocytes with an organic compound to produce liquid lysate from the amebocytes that contained all the secrets of the horseshoe's defense mechanism against endotoxins. If you dropped a bit of medicine into that lysate, you could examine it a few hours later for the tell-tale gel that signaled coagulation and provided proof that a sample was contaminated.

The road ahead for the LAL test was full of twists, turns, and bureaucratic setbacks. But Levin's LAL innovation passed each new test thrown in its path and finally emerged as the gold standard in endotoxin testing in the 1970s. It became official standard operating procedure in the 1980s, some three decades after Frederik Bang decided to spend a part of his summer taking a "naive" look at the blood of a prehistoric sea creature.

Levin has received numerous honors over the years for the run of discovery and innovation that led to the invention of the Limulus amebocyte lysate test. In 2019, the American Association for the Advancement of Science gave him its Golden Goose Award. Fittingly, that prize celebrates the way basic and often unfocused research into natural phenomena—the stuff that we all make fun of on occasion as wasted money—can sometimes yield great dividends for human health and wellness.

Maintaining a Natural Balance

Limulus polyphemus has been through tough times over its 450-million-year existence. The species has survived as many as five different mass-extinction events. More recent challenges arose by way of humankind. In the late 1800s, horseshoe crabs became a popular agricultural fertilizer and livestock feed. Historical photos show farm fields near the Delaware Bay blanketed with thousands upon thousands of *Limulus* carcasses.

That threat eased as better, cheaper fertilizers came on the scene. Another threat arose in the 1980s with the increasing popularity of conch and eel in regional cuisines in various parts of the world. Horseshoe crabs are commonly used as bait in both of those fisheries. Another challenge lies in the way residential and/ or commercial development can encroach on or disrupt horseshoe crab habitats.

Is modern medical science and its LAL test a threat as well, especially given the recent need to test billions of doses of COVID vaccines? The answer to that question is counterintuitive. Jim Cooper has been involved with the LAL testing industry since the 1970s, when he played a key role in shepherding the test out of the laboratory and into the marketplace.

"The COVID vaccines are really just a drop in the bucket," he says. "That can be hard for people to get their heads around if they don't know how this industry works, but it's true."

The way the industry works begins with a fishing boat. Specially trained and equipped crews catch horseshoes at night-time in the warmer months. The work is done in catch-and-release fashion by rules Cooper helped to establish in the 1970s. Once on shore, the crabs are trucked to nearby laboratories where blood is slowly drawn from each individual for about five minutes. By rule, crabs must be returned to the water alive within 36 hours—usually, it happens in less than a day.

About 450,000 horseshoes are temporarily harvested this way yearly. Most of those crabs do just fine, but some die as a result of the ordeal. Mortality rates from bleeding are difficult to measure precisely after crabs return to the wild, but the top-end number most widely accepted by researchers is 15 percent. That adds up to a number of deaths much, much smaller than the tolls inflicted by the bait industry and by natural attrition due to predators, disease, and old age.

The Atlantic horseshoe crab population has been listed as "vulnerable" by the International Union for Conservation of Nature across a broad range stretching from the Gulf of Mexico to the northeastern United States. But there has been good news in Delaware Bay, where the population seems to have stabilized after a sharp decline in the early 1990s. Numbers of spawning females counted in annual surveys have been on the rise since the early 2000s.

One thing working in the crabs' favor is the fact that Limulus blood now ranks as an indispensable tool in protecting human health. Their newfound importance has spurred numerous efforts to study and protect the species. The surveys that are now conducted annually didn't happen in pre-LAL times. The bait fishery has been outlawed in South Carolina and operates under new, stricter limits in New Jersey, Delaware, Maryland, and other states. Bird lovers concerned about the health of those migrating shorebirds also contribute to the push for best practices, as they want to ensure the future health of a horseshoe population that provides their beloved birds with critical food during migration times.

A little *Limulus* blood goes a long way. The blood collected from those harvested crabs is transformed into 70 million units of a 21st-century version of the lysate invented by Levin. It goes even further because of the way LAL tests are conducted—not on individual vials, or even on vats of medicine but rather in spot-test fashion at manufacturing facilities. Small numbers of tests actually clear vast quantities of product.

"Think about walking down a hospital corridor and seeing all the IV bags, all the medicines being injected," Cooper says. "Then think about all the hospitals, pharmacies, and clinics across the country—and around much of the world." Those 70 million LAL test units were enough to ensure the safety of that global supply chain before the COVID pandemic. The rise in test kits necessitated by the arrival of new vaccines is, as Levin puts it, "really quite minimal." Especially when compared with a benefit measured in millions of lives and countless cases of disease.

FEATS!

Is That a Piece of Pittsville in Your Pocket?

The next time you fish around in your pocket or purse for some change, give some thought to the humble quarter. Yes, that's an image of George Washington on the head's side. But is it also the image of Dexter Truitt?

That question doesn't have a definitive answer, but it will lead us along a fun, follow-the-breadcrumbs trail. A native of little Pittsville on Maryland's Eastern Shore, Truitt became an actor and moved to California. He was pretty well known in his early 20th century day as a George Washington lookalike and impersonator.

His friends and family say that he sat as a model for the sculptor who created the image on the quarter. No proof of this has turned up, but tantalizing tidbits appear along that breadcrumb trail indicating that the Truitt legend might be true. We'll pick up that trail in Pittsville, one in the run of one-horse towns along the Route 50 highway between Salisbury and Ocean City.

From Dirt Crossroads to Trains Full of Strawberries
Pittsville wasn't officially incorporated until 1906, but its story goes back before that. Europeans were late to arrive on this part of the Eastern Shore. The earliest "land patents" date to the middle 1700s. The landscape that greeted those settlers was different in colonial times, much of it swampy and uninviting.

The names those early landowners gave their "patents" are fascinating, hinting at the dreams and fears of folks who risked everything by moving into what was then a sparsely populated wilderness. One is "A Gift to My First Son." Others are "Newfound Land," "Hardship," and "Tribulation." Then there is "Bald Cypress," which points toward the environmental changes that would unfold as Europeans grew in number. That swamp-loving tree once abounded here, but the damp cypress forests would eventually get cut down and transformed into shingles and other products. Slowly but surely, swampy forests became farmland.

Growth was a gradual affair. The first record showing a house on land that would become part of Pittsville dates to 1810. A store opened soon after. It wasn't until 1840 that there were enough people around to start up a Methodist congregation. The town was called "Derickson's Crossroads" at that point.

The name Pittsville came by way of the railroad. That steam-powered miracle of 19th century technology arrived shortly after the Civil War. A local physician named Hilary Pitts served as president of the Wicomico and Pocomoke Railroad, which is how his name ended up on the new railroad station. Over time, it spilled out to encompass the whole town.

The railroad brought monumental changes, just as it did in countless other Delmarva locales. Everybody in and around Pittsville went crazy for the strawberry business once those highly profitable fruits could make the trip by rail to Wilmington, Philadelphia, and even New York City before going bad. The strawberry boom in Pittsville lasted for decades. At its peak, fiftysome rail cars rolled out of town every day during the spring harvest.

That fueled serious growth at last. By the start of the 1880s, Pittsville had three grocery/general stores and three lumber companies. There was a hotel, too. Those aforementioned Methodists seem to have amassed a lot of power. Concerned about the moral and physical well-being of the local populace, they pushed through a law shutting down all three of the town's taverns.

Dexter Truitt's Journey to Hollywood

Dexter Truitt was born during the early, heady days of that strawberry upswing, on Sept. 13, 1888. Aside from that date, I haven't come across any breadcrumbs that reveal details about his family background and childhood years.

But there's no doubt about his birthplace, as that's what Truitt wrote on his registration paperwork for the military draft in World War I. He filed that document in June 1917, giving his father's name as Joseph L. Truitt. By that point, Dexter was a widower with one child living on North 34th Street in Philadelphia. He describes himself as a man of medium build, with gray eyes and black hair. He was working in the produce business.

Much later, in 1934, Truitt applied for "Veterans Compensation" from the government for his service during World War I. According to that document, he served from 1917 to 1919, spending much of that time overseas in the 312th Field Artillery Battery of the Army's 79th Infantry Division. He fought in the infamously brutal Meuse-Argonne offensive, suffering injuries from mustard gas and two gunshot wounds, one in his right leg and the other in his left shoulder. He was discharged from Camp Dix, New Jersey on June 6, 1919.

The record on that widower-with-a-child business is vague. The *Salisbury Daily Times* looked into this topic in 2002 and reported that Truitt had married a local girl from Mardela Springs. The story doesn't give her name, but it reports that she died while giving birth to a boy named Floyd who was then raised by Truitt's in-laws. Floyd eventually became known locally by the nickname of "Sparky."

Somewhere after his return from overseas service, Truitt set his sights on an acting career. A snippet of oral history from Pittsville says this adventure began on a whim, when he entered an acting contest for amateurs and came out a winner. He moved to Los Angeles in the mid-1920s, landing film and theatrical roles under the stage name David Ward. Along the way he became quite well known for his resemblance to George Washington, appearing at various civic and charity events in the persona of the Father of Our Country.

The *Hollywood Daily Citizen*, March 3, 1927: *David Ward, national impersonator of George Washington, will appear in costume [at an upcoming civic event]. The double of the Virginia planter has similar features, is the same height, carries the same weight, wears the same size shoes, gloves, other apparel. For seven years he has been entertaining groups with his work.*

The *Minneapolis Star-Tribune*, Oct. 28, 1928: *David Ward, America's foremost impersonator of George Washington, was selected by [the film director] Erich von Stroheim [to portray] a typical Austrian soldier and [appeared] throughout [a film titled The Wedding March] as a member of Emperor Franz Joseph's famous Life Guard Mounted.*

The director posed with Ward/Truitt for a fun publicity photo showing both men in fancy-schmancy military garb. The handwritten caption on the back reads:

Erich von Stroheim, director, star and author of the forthcoming Paramount picture, The Wedding March, *with David Ward, foremost impersonator of George Washington. ... In "The Wedding March," Ward appears not as George Washington, but as an Austrian soldier.*

That silent film is worth a quick detour, as it's a famous example of Hollywood excess. It was originally budgeted at $300,000. The producers shut filming down when expenses reached $1.25 million. The Wikipedia entry on *The Wedding March* gives examples of the extravagance and includes a memorable quote from the director:

Stroheim rebuilt huge sets for St. Stephen's Cathedral, the streets surrounding it, various palatial rooms, and an entire apple orchard with thousands of blossoms individually tied to the trees. Stroheim defended his elaborate set choices by stating, "They say I give them sewers—and dead cats! This time I am giving them beauty. Beauty—and apple blossoms! More than they can stand!"

The name "David Ward" pops up now and again in cast lists for plays, but I haven't found a lot of references to movie roles. One 1926 newspaper story announces that Ward will have a role in the then-upcoming Cecil B. DeMille production, *King of Kings*, but Ward's name doesn't appear in the final cast list. Perhaps his part was too brief for that, or perhaps it ended up on the cutting-room floor.

Several old newspaper stories from the 1920s say that Ward portrayed Washington on film multiple times, but I haven't been able to pin down details on those movies. Oral history back home on the Eastern Shore supports the idea that Dexter Truitt found his way into the movies with some frequency. In that 2002 *Salisbury Daily Times* article, the actor's nephew, Gerald Truitt

Jr., is quoted as saying that people from Pittsville would travel to Salisbury movie theaters every time their town's native son appeared on the big screen. That local grapevine says that Truitt played in so many westerns he earned the nickname "Tex."

Truitt appeared in his Washington garb at countless civic events. He gave talks. He marched in parades. He made appearances at charity galas. He engaged with young people through groups such as the Boy Scouts and the Campfire Girls. He once told the *Los Angeles Evening Express* newspaper that impersonating Washington for these audiences was something he regarded as a "sacred privilege."

I have never attempted to bring [Washington] before my audiences as a "plaster saint," but as a real man, a man among men, ... a man loved and revered by his comrades, a man worthy of the ideals surrounding his memory. [My goal is to] arouse to some degree these ideals in the boyhood and manhood of America.

A Second Family, a Dreadful Accident, an Early Demise

I am not sure when Dexter Truitt got married for a second time. He had three more children with Sarah Lafferty Truitt. On that 1934 paperwork he filed seeking veteran's compensation, he lists 13-year-old Nancy, 11-year-old Helen, and nine-year-old Elsie in addition to that son from his first marriage, 18-year-old Floyd.

Truitt retired from acting in 1935 and moved to Tujunga, a little way north of Los Angeles. Brand new at the time, the community was a planned affair built on utopian dreams as a place where folks could escape city life and get back to self-sufficiency and living off of the land. Tujunga drew lots of World War I veterans seeking refuge from the high rents and other big-city complications of Los Angeles.

You Wouldn't Believe!

It was an idiosyncratic town. One prominent Main Street business was named "Dean's store, the locale of the 'Millionaire's Club of Happiness and Contentment.'" The town's marketing slogan was, "Move to Tujunga with a trowel and a bag of cement, and build your own." Many residents did just that, constructing their own houses, keeping livestock, and working small plots of farmland. There were cattle at the Ward/Truitt house on Mountair Avenue.

Alas, Truitt didn't get the chance to enjoy the utopian dream of Tujunga for long. He died in 1944. He was in his mid-50s. His obituaries say that he had suffered a terrible fall three years before that left him physically incapacitated.

Is That Really a Guy from Pittsville on the Quarter?

OK, about that quarter business. The evidence in favor of this includes oral history from Pittsville and the Truitt family, newspaper mentions across various decades, and the direct words of a Hollywood celebrity.

Let's start with that last one. Truitt was friends with the novelist James M. Cain. Cain's best-known work is *The Postman Always Rings Twice*. His *Double Indemnity* and *Mildred Pierce* were turned into films, too. He also wrote screenplays—all told, he had a hand in 20-plus Hollywood films over the years.

Cain and Truitt became friends in the Army. Perhaps they bonded over shared ties to Maryland and the Eastern Shore. Born in Annapolis in 1892, Cain moved with his parents to Chestertown, Md. in 1903. He graduated from Washington College. He worked as a reporter in Baltimore before hitting it big in novels and movies.

In 1944, Cain wrote a letter to Truitt's son, Floyd. That was the same year Dexter Truitt died, so it must have been written either while the Pittsville native was on his deathbed, or shortly after his demise. Cain seems to be recounting the history of their friendship. I haven't seen the whole letter, just references to and quotes from it. Here is a Cain quote by way of a newspaper article about a long-ago visit he had paid to Truitt:

He was the same genial, friendly, unabashedly outrageous fellow I had liked so well. I sat looking at him in my living room, noting at once something I hadn't observed in the Army—the startling resemblance to George Washington.

Cain says in the letter that Truitt later told him he'd been the model for the image of Washington on the quarter. Interestingly, Cain's collected papers offer a hint that Truitt tried his hand at writing, in addition to acting. Those papers are housed at the Library of Congress, where an online summary of contents includes lots of works by lots of writers who submitted their work for Cain's review. One listing: "Flame of Louisiana (Well of Enchantment)," by Dexter Truitt.

Folks back home in Pittsville heard about the quarter business, too. Residents and former residents alike have told reporters many times over the years that Truitt did that modeling duty. It's presented as fact in the well-done booklet *Pittsville: A Pictorial History.*

Truitt's widow, Sarah, said the same thing to the writers who prepared her husband's obituary. Here is how it appeared in the *Los Angeles Times*:

Mr. Truitt, whose marked physical resemblance to the first president brought him from his Maryland home to Hollywood, ... sat as a model for the head of Washington that appears on the quarter, his widow ... recalled. He also played the part [of Washington] in numerous films before retiring to raise cattle in 1935.

The *New York Times*, along with quite a few other papers,

included the same information, attributed each time to Sarah Truitt.

This all seems quite reliable, doesn't it? Truitt, his family, his friends, his hometown acquaintances—everyone says it happened. The rub here is a lack of official proof. If you ask historians at the American Numismatic Association about Dexter Truitt and the quarter, they will start sounding like the CIA, saying something along the lines of "we can neither confirm nor deny …" This isn't because of some secrecy thing—it's just that they have no official records of Truitt playing a role in the creation of the coin.

The quarter came into being in 1932 to commemorate the bicentennial of Washington's birth. The image of Washington used on that coin was the work of a prolific New York sculptor, John Flanagan. Official records say only that Flanagan based his design on a famous 1785 bust of Washington by the French sculptor Jean-Antoine Houdon. Those records make no mention of Dexter Truitt or David Ward any other model visiting Flanagan's studio during the creative process.

But by the time Flanagan was creating the quarter image in 1932, Truitt had a national reputation for his uncanny resemblance to Washington. It would have been an easy matter for Flanagan to reach out to him, or, perhaps, for Flanagan to recognize the possibilities after a chance social encounter. There was a lot of overlap in those days between Hollywood and the New York theater and art worlds—actors were often shuttling between the two coasts. David Ward might have been in the neighborhood for an audition or role while Flanagan was working on the quarter in his New York studio.

We'll probably never know with 100 percent certainty, but if I were a betting man, my money would go with the oral and community histories here, especially considering the way those reports come from multiple sources all saying the same thing. None of those people were getting money or other goodies out of the deal. You probably really are carrying around a little piece of Pittsville in your purse or pocket.

Postscript of Gratitude

I need to give credit here to the Secrets of the Eastern Shore community on Facebook. As anyone familiar with that page knows, I post a lot of photos and facts about days gone by on the Delmarva Peninsula. Sometimes I get things wrong, but readers there always seem to have my back, kindly alerting me to mistakes or telling me about typos and oversights.

When I first posted about Dexter Truitt and the quarter, it was short and sweet. I was reporting that the booklet *Pittsville: A Pictorial History* says the story is true. One reader got a little indignant about this, demanding that I provide hard proof.

I happened to be traveling that day, so I was offline. That Secrets of the Eastern Shore community leaped into action. The volunteer or staffer who was working social media for the Nabb Center for Delmarva History and Culture spent time wandering the internet, then posted Truitt's World War I draft paperwork and his later request for veteran's compensation. A reader named Wayne Cannon found Truitt's obit in the *New York Times* and posted that. Folks in Pittsville chimed in with their two cents on local oral histories. One of them, Christopher Travers, reported that Dexter Truitt's "grandson was my roommate." Pictures of Truitt's grave in California appeared. So did a photo of Truitt hanging out with James M. Cain.

Bottom line: We have fun on that page. You should follow it if you don't already: Facebook.com/SecretsoftheEasternShore.

CLARISSA & DEWLIP: A MOST EXCELLENT ADVENTURE

To appreciate this little anecdote, you'll need to imagine yourself in the shoes of a precocious 11-year-old girl. Her name is Clarissa. One of her favorite companions is a little dachshund named Dewlip. The year is 1913.

Big things were happening that year in Clarissa's neighborhood, a stretch of Maryland's Eastern Shore called Miles River Neck. If you leave the Talbot County seat of Easton today heading for the town of St. Michaels, you'll come to a traffic light at Unionville Road. Take that to the right (northbound), and you'll soon rise up and over the Miles River by way of a bridge that delivers sweet views of the water and the ruins of an old church.

The current bridge—it went up in the 1980s—is the third span over this stretch of the Miles. The first, a clattering wooden affair built in the 1850s, lasted fiftysome years before it was closed to traffic over safety concerns. A ferry operation filled the gap until a new bridge could be built.

The big happening in Clarissa's neighborhood in Novem-

ber 1913 was the opening of that second bridge. She'd seen all
the construction crews. She'd heard adults talk about the upcoming grand opening. And somewhere along the line, she got a half-
crazy notion into her head.

'A Miracle of Modern Engineering'

In his 1984 book, *Talbot County: A History*, the late historian
Dickson Preston reports that this second Miles River bridge was
regarded as a "miracle of modern engineering" thanks to newfangled concrete-and-steel construction methods that involved nearly
5,000 tons of "reinforced concrete piles, floor slabs, abutments,
and piers." The 40-foot-long, bascule-style draw was new-
fangled, too—it rose up and down instead of swinging sideways
the way other drawbridges did in those days. Newspaper reports
marveled as well over the way electric and telephone wires were
threaded through the interior guts of the structure, invisible to
passersby outside.

When opening day arrived on Nov. 1, construction bigwigs from all over Maryland and nearby states came out to gawk
at the groundbreaking structure. So, too, did local and regional
dignitaries.

The *Baltimore Evening Sun* reported that the ceremonies
began "promptly at 8 o'clock." A local dignitary, Anna Earle,
was awarded the honor of being the first person to cross. She was
the matron of a nearby historic estate known as The Anchorage.
Accompanying her was the chief construction engineer, Henry
Wilcox. They made the crossing in what Preston describes as a
"cutaway carriage."

According to the *Evening Sun*, a crowd of "spectators
cheered as Miss Earle reached the road upon the far side of the
bridge." But the reporter who wrote that missed the best part of

the story. According to Preston's book, Earle and Wilcox did not actually have the honor of being the first across:

Eleven-year-old Clarissa Tilghman Goldsborough had beaten [them] to it. Even before the formal ceremony began, ... she rode across the bridge on her bicycle. With her was her dachshund, Dewlip, who pulled a wooden cart containing her doll.

Postscript: What Happened to Clarissa?

Clarissa lived to the ripe old age of 95. She married a Baltimore attorney in 1933, becoming Clarissa Tilghman Yost. They lived in the Bolton Hill neighborhood of that city for many years before returning to Clarissa's childhood home, a Talbot County estate known as Ferrybridge Farm. She was active in historic preservation with the Colonial Dames of America and the Historical Society of Talbot County. I wonder how often she bragged in those later years about how she had stolen her own little moment of history, with help from little Dewlip.

Oh, how I wish someone had taken a photo of that scene!

THE AMERICAN THEATER WAS BORN IN PUNGOTEAGUE?

Everybody's a critic. But not everybody's a critic on the level of Edward Martin.

On a summer night in 1665, he ventured out to Fowkes Tavern near Pungoteague, Va. and found himself watching two actors put on an entertainment called "Ye Bare and Ye Cubbe." Translation: "The Bear and the Cub."

Two things make Martin's seemingly mundane outing worth our attention. First, the show is the first appearance in the historical record of a theatrical performance in the colonies—yup, the American theater was born on Virginia's Eastern Shore on Aug. 27, 1665. Second, that same occasion marks the birth of American theater criticism.

To say that Edward Martin did not enjoy the show would be an understatement. Lacking the ability to pick up his cell phone and vent on Facebook or Twitter, he elected to march over to the local magistrate's office and demand that everyone involved in the production be arrested. The accusation was "public wickedness," a colorful legal term that was used back then, basically, as a synonym for blasphemy.

That magistrate did what Martin asked. Actors Cornelius Watkinson and Phillip Howard were tossed in jail. So was the playwright, William Darby. All three were held there for at least a little while. It's unclear when they managed to post bail and regain their freedom while awaiting trial.

The Plot Is a Mystery

Most folks who've looked into this think that Edward Martin was a Quaker, which means he was a member of what was then a tiny religious minority on the Anglican-dominated Virginia shore. There is no surviving record of the details in his complaint, just as there is no surviving script or even plot description for "Ye Bare and Ye Cubbe."

Various historians have done bits of guesswork about this. One, Joel Eis, chalks it up to politics. He speculates that the play had anti-British undertones that touched on tensions between an upper class that was hyper loyal to England and middle-class merchants who were angry about restrictions placed by the king on the international tobacco trade. To bolster this theory, Eis goes so far as to find a string of pamphlets and speeches from those days that employ the same brand of "parent-fledgling analogy" in the play's title as a way to criticize the English.

Another theory puts religion front and center, arguing that Martin may have been arguing that theatrical performances were sinful in and of themselves. At first glance, this might make Pungoteague look backward and intolerant. After all, the date here is half a century past the death of William Shakespeare, whose productions were quite popular back in the mother country during the Bard's own lifetime.

But the picture is more complicated. Shakespeare died in

1616, but a religiously based backlash against the theater erupted in England starting in the late 1600s. Clergyman Jeremy Collier wrote an influential book-length diatribe that (according to historian David Manning) describes theatrical performances as endeavors "where playwright, player, and audience [meet] to collude in sin" and concludes that "audience appreciation of these plays [is] tantamount to worshipping the Devil."

In actuality, the mere fact that a play was staged in Pungoteague as far back as 1665 puts Virginia's Eastern Shore closer to the ranks of open-minded than intolerant. Up in New England, for instance, the Puritans and other Congregationalist sects put plays in the same category as entertainments like cockfighting and boxing, as "forms of levity and mirth [that lead] easily to sin." They feared that such "public amusements" would infect the "entire community with the corrupt tastes of a few individuals." As late as 1767, the Massachusetts Assembly would outlaw theater shows altogether.

Perhaps Martin's objection was as simple as the play being performed on Sunday, the Sabbath. Or perhaps it went deeper—was the content somehow rebellious or sacrilegious? There is a third possibility, too. Some researchers who've dug into the "Ye Bare and Ye Cubbe" controversy suspect that the case wasn't really about the theater at all. What Martin was really up to in this view was getting Watkinson, Howard, and Darby in trouble, over some personal matter. In other words: Perhaps he used public doubts about the morality of the theater as a prop in his own revenge drama.

The Critic Gets a Drubbing

The case has a happy ending. But first, an entertaining detour. This "Bare and Cubbe" contretemps arose a short handful of decades after the beginnings of the Jamestown settlement. Virginia still didn't have much in the way of governmental infrastructure. For instance, Accomack County had no courthouse in 1665.

Instead, itinerant judges heard cases in private homes or makeshift public spaces. In the case of "Ye Bare and Ye Cubbe," the hearing unfolded at the scene of the alleged crime, right back in Fowkes Tavern. To add an additional twist, the defendants were ordered to show up wearing "those habilments that they then acted in, and give a draught of such verses or other Speeches and passages, which were then acted by them."

Translation: Let's put on the show again!

The playwright and actors performed their play in court on Dec. 18, 1665. The judges saw no evidence of the "public wickedness" that Martin had complained about. Martin didn't even show up to watch the proceedings and testify. Those judges demanded that he show up soon and provide them an explanation of his actions.

Martin appeared on Jan. 16, 1666. This time, it was the judges who played the roles of harsh critics. Here is their ruling (if reading 17th century prose gives you a headache, just skip the next paragraph):

Whereas Edward Martin was this Day examined Concerning his information given to Mr. Fawsett his Majestie's Attorney for Accomac County about a play called the Bare and the Cubb, whereby several persons were brought to Court and Charges theron arise from the Court find the said persons not guilty of same suspended the payment of Court Charges, and for as much as it appeareth upon the oath of the said Mr. Fawsett that upon the said Edward Martin's informacon the charge and trouble of that suit did accrew, Its ordered that the said Edward Martin pay all the charges in the suit.

You Wouldn't Believe!

Translation: The charges against the theater troupe were dismissed. Edward Martin was ordered to pay everyone's court costs. That's where the judicial trail runs cold. There is no record of whether Martin actually paid up, or of any other aspect of the case going forward.

Postscript: A Modern Twist
The tale of "Ye Bare and Ye Cubbe" has dropped into obscurity over the years, though it's still written about now and again in the nerdiest reaches of theater history studies. The lack of solid information in the historical record means it's hard to draw big sweeping conclusions from the incident about the arts or jurisprudence of early colonial America.

But the play has had a few moments in the sun. In 2007, the Historic Jamestown tourist attraction put on a made-up modern version play, in which the plot was built around that bit of guesswork that it had revolutionary anti-British content. That production was revived a few years ago by North Street Playhouse in Onancock.

The one remnant of the play's significance that's always available lies along the backroads of Virginia's Eastern Shore. The next time you are traveling that way, find your way to Bobtown Road, then slow down as you get a little way below Pungoteague, near the intersection with Michaels Hill Road. There, an old-school sign marks the onetime site of Fowkes Tavern, home to the "first recorded play in English America"—the opening scene in a much larger story that runs right up to the bright lights of Broadway.

A Birth of Freedom in Eastville

NOTE: My other books include lots of wondrous tales from days gone by. This excerpt from Eastern Shore Road Trips #2: 26 MORE One-Day Adventures on Delmarva *is one piece in a larger excursion titled "Eastville, Va. & Savage Neck."*

Eastville's pretty Courthouse Green has been at the center of life in the seat of Northampton County, Va. since way back in 1715. Court cases were being heard near here even before that, actually—starting in 1677, sessions were held at the long-gone home of a man named Henry Matthews.

The Green is chock full of interesting old buildings. The older of the two courthouses here went up in the 1730s. After a second courthouse went up, that first one morphed for a while into a tavern. The "new" courthouse on the Green dates to 1899. Inside, the clerk's office houses the longest continuous set of court records anywhere in the country, dating back to the 1630s. One reason those records remain is that local officials in Civil War times studiously ignored an order from the state that all important paperwork be transported to the state capital of Richmond, which would soon be burned by Union troops.

As a result, visitors today can review records that include the marks of Indian chiefs and a document sealing the deal on a property transfer involving none other than Daniel Boone. Back outside, you'll also find an Old Clerk's Office (1830s), a Debtor's Prison (1814), and a Confederate monument (1914) on the Green.

A Declaration Before Its Time

Freedom is a word worth thinking about while wandering around here. Take a minute to imagine the scene that unfolded on Aug. 3, 1776 when a messenger arrived in town after a month-long ride from Philadelphia. The copy of the Declaration of Independence he had in his saddlebag was read aloud to the populace from the courthouse steps.

But Eastville also has an earlier claim to revolutionary fame. The context of that claim is a complicated affair, tied up in a messy bit of regime change back in England as well as contentious local debates over dealing with Indians. Here's the quick version: Virginia began life as a private enterprise ruled by soldiers in military fashion, then morphed into something more traditionally colonial as the royal powers that be in England asserted control. Virginians had a measure of autonomy in that arrangement through the so-called House of Burgesses.

Formed in 1619, the first democratically elected legislative body in the American colonies was set up to include members from various geographic regions, including Northampton County. But colonial leaders on the western shore ignored this little detail in the late 1640s, when the House of Burgesses went right ahead passing laws and imposing taxes despite the fact that no one had been elected or appointed during those years to represent the people of Northampton.

Eventually, the locals decided they'd had enough. The last straw came with the imposition of a stiff new tax on tobacco. On March 30, 1652, county leaders penned what is in retrospect a truly incredible letter:

Forasmuch as wee had neither summons for Ellecton of Burgesses nor voyce in their Assemblie ... wee conceive that wee may Lawfullie ptest agt the pceedings in the Act of Assemlie for public Taxacons ...

Fight through that old language and those odd spellings, and you will get to the bottom line: No taxation without representation, please.

This "Northampton Protest" was the first time anyone went public with such a complaint in the colonies—remarkably, it happened 124 years before the Declaration of Independence and nearly four decades before the same concept was first spelled out across the Atlantic in the landmark English Bill of Rights of 1689. The protest was a success, by the way—those western shore leaders waved a white flag and agreed to most of Northampton's demands.

BOOM & BUST!

BLACK GOLD IN PARSONSBURG!

If some TV producer made an Eastern Shore version of *The Beverly Hillbillies*, the family at the center of things would need to hail from Parsonsburg, Md. In the early 1900s, that sleepy town east of Salisbury was the epicenter of the Great Delmarva Oil Craze.

How big was this "Craze?" In 1914 the brand new Wicomico Oil & Gas Co. took out ads in regional newspapers looking for investors. Those ads described the stakes as a "Business Proposition fraught with possibilities so big" that they might lead to the creation of "one of Maryland's richest industries."

That would be "bubbling' crude," "Black Gold," "Texas Tea"–all those synonyms for oil that pop up in the "Beverly Hillbillies" theme song. Shares cost $1 a pop. The ad promised that an "investment today of $50 might mean for you an independent income" for life!" Be warned, however: "Tomorrow may be too late."

If scientific research [and the] expert opinion of experienced oilmen and mining engineers count for anything, the Parsonsburg Ridge is rich in deposits of crude petroleum. ... Prove your patriotism and business acumen by subscribing today for as many shares as you can afford.

Pay Heed to the Fog

You are probably shaking your head right now: Who would believe such nonsense?

The answer to that question runs into the tens of thousands. Folks from all over the country bought into the Delmarva oil hype. Something to think about: Among those multitudes of investors were quite a few people who were just as smart and capable as you and I, maybe even more so. It's easy to look back and laugh at a turn of events like the Delmarva Oil Craze. What's more interesting is trying to see things through the eyes of people living in the moment, who had no way of knowing what the future would hold. Here is how the famous fiction writer Milan Kundera put that challenge:

Man proceeds in the fog. But when he looks back to judge people of the past, he sees no fog on their path. From his present, which was their faraway future, their path looks perfectly clear to him, good visibility all the way. Looking back, he sees the path, he sees the people proceeding, he sees their mistakes, but not the fog.

In the Beginning: Farmers Having a Gas

This strange chapter in Delmarva history begins with a comic turn. Here is the sequence:

• Around 1900 a farmer named "Mr. White" sunk a well three miles north of Parsonsburg. He heard a strange gurgling noise as he went about that work, but he didn't bother to try and figure out what caused it.

• A few years later, farmer John W. Wimbrow dug a well. At 36 feet, he heard a gurgling. Then, much to his surprise, he struck a volume of flammable gas that kept spouting and spout-ing, no end in sight.

• Word got around. Mr. White remembered how his well had once gurgled. Other farmers started talking about the various gurgling sounds they'd heard over the years.

• Everyone wondered: How much gas was down there?

• Wimbrow hooked up a pipe, ran it into his house, and used the gas to fuel his stove. His daughter, Mrs. Jessie Johnson, testified later that "the flame was so hot in our cookstove that it would boil a kettle of water in three minutes."

• At first, these were just fun times. Wimbrow jerry-rigged a fancy gas lamp for his dining room. Other farmers dug out con-nections to underground gas and hooked up this, that, or another household gadget. Robert Smith went so far as to rig up a gas-powered street lamp in front of his house.

Word spread to neighboring towns, then beyond. In *Wicomico County: A History*, George H. Corddry quotes one resi-dent's recollection of those heady early days of the Oil Craze:

The Baltimore, Chesapeake & Atlantic Railway arranged weekly excursions from Claiborne, Easton, Salisbury, and Ocean City. Curious spectators flocked to the well by the trainload, and Mr. Wimbrow had a control valve placed on the well so that he could turn on the gas, light it, and explain the entire procedure to the visitors.

From Slick Gimmick to Crude Dreams

By 1910, things had taken a serious turn. All these gassy events sparked questions. Might there be enough gas down there to pro-vide power to all of Parsonsburg? Might there be enough to run a pipeline to Salisbury and turn a profit?

Could the potential be even bigger? Would this discovery

follow a pattern seen recently in Pennsylvania, West Virginia, Ohio, and Texas? First comes the discovery of gas, and then comes the discovery of crude oil. Could Parsonsburg become a Delmarva version of Beaumont, Tex., where, in 1901, the "Lucas gusher" at the world-famous Spindletop well had launched the Texas oil boom?

Before Spindletop erupted, the so-called experts had all scoffed at the notion that Texas would ever become a big oil producer.

The first company to nose around what soon became known as the "Parsonsburg Ridge" was the Maryland Oil & Gas Company. In August 1910, the *Baltimore Sun* reported that this newly formed firm had signed conditional drilling leases covering 8,000 acres. The leases would kick in if and when a gusher of gas or oil turned up. The company set up shop on the Wimbrow farm to run a preliminary test:

An experiment was made with the gas as an illuminant. In its raw state the flame is blue and the candle-power is not high. When mixed with air and used with a mantle, a wonderfully fine light is produced.

The firm then moved a "pile-driving rig" onto Wimbrow's property and sank a cylinder into the ground, collecting gas from deeper down and sending it out for chemical analysis.

In another story that same week, the *Sun* relayed rumors about how oilmen from West Virginia and other "foreign" locales were wandering Wicomico and Worcester counties, chatting with farmers and studying the landscape. These out-of-towners did not seem overly concerned about the fact that Maryland Oil and Gas had a head start:

"There is plenty in the field for all," one of them said.

That week's newspaper stories also included speculation

71

about how carbon-laden "ancient forests" might have been hermetically sealed under Delmarva clay in a geological phenomenon known from elsewhere in the world to create major oil and gas deposits. One note of skepticism did appear near the end of one of these stories:

The neighborhood is divided as to what the gas is. Some say it is real natural gas and others incline to the belief that it is a big deposit of marsh gas.

That latter type would almost certainly run out before anyone got rich.

The Experts Step Up on Parsonsburg Ridge

By the end of 1910, the Craze was picking up steam. The *Baltimore Sun*:

Land in the vicinity of Parsonsburg has gone out of reach in price, and residents of that section are sanguine of success that oil or gas will be found.

Remember my warning about the fog? This really did look like more than a pipe dream, especially to folks who put their trust in expert opinion and scientific predictions. Early on, the Maryland Geological Survey predicted that "oil and gas in large quantities" would "probably" turn up. One of the country's biggest oil companies, Pure, sent in-house expert A.L. Bates to Parsonsburg. The *Oil and Gas Journal* reported:

Mr. Bates seems to be much impressed with the possibility of finding oil in this county, and as he is a man of large experience, his opinion should be worthy of respect.

The article went on to hint strongly that Bates was negotiating leases with local farmers on Pure's behalf. Such negotiations by other companies had already spread out of Wicomico and Worcester counties and up into Southern Delaware.

You Wouldn't Believe!

Next up was the industry's biggest celebrity. Anthony Francis Lucas was to crude oil back then what Bill Gates is to our modern computers. His incredible strike at the Spindletop well in Texas had captured worldwide attention. Here is the *Baltimore Sun*, paraphrasing Lucas after conducting an interview with him based on his in-person tour of the area:

The evidence of prospects [is] better in this particular field than that which led him to discover in Texas the Beaumont section of the famous Lucas gusher.

A charismatic Croatian immigrant, Lucas speculated that the Parsonsburg Ridge lay atop a magnificent subterranean river of oil that ran from Pennsylvania down to Alabama. Both those states had booming new oil industries in those years. This long run of optimistic judgments from top-of-the-line experts led to summaries of the situation like this one from the *Oil and Gas Journal:*

A successful strike [at Parsonsburg] ... would cause a wave of prosperity to sweep over this section which would be phenomenal in its scope. There seems to be more reason to hope for success with every new venture which is opened up here, and within a short time it may be possible for us to chronicle something of a definite nature which would be of everlasting benefit to this community.

The *Wilmington Evening Journal* soon reported that "confidence in gas and oil prospects [in and around Parsonsburg] has become so strong" that even the most conservative of businessmen were quite eager to buy into stock offerings of newly created oil companies.

The Voice in the Wilderness
There's a naysayer in every crowd, isn't there? In this case, the

Maryland Geological Survey stepped into the role of doubting Thomas. Early on, that state agency had expressed high hopes about the gas in Parsonsburg, but they changed their tune as time went by. A brief write-up on the prospects for Parsonsburg in the 1918 edition of the *Surface and Underground Water Resources of Maryland* consisted of one red flag after another.

For starters, the evidence that had everyone excited came from shallow wells, while big strikes always arose from deeper down. Such "surface indications" are notoriously unreliable, the report warned, and "would, if relied upon, lead to some very expensive and probably disappointing ventures." In addition, chemical analysis of the Parsonsburg gas revealed only one form of hydrocarbon, methane. The gas in productive strikes elsewhere around the country contained multiple different hydrocarbons. The bottom line:

> *[This] suggests that [the Parsonsburg] gas comes from ... a pool of marsh gas and not a deep-seated, large pool of gas or oil.*

Translation: There was no vast "river of oil" under the Delmarva Peninsula.

The End: Going Out with a Whimper

There's not much more to the story. Folks spent a lot of time and money, but all they learned was that the few doubting Thomases out there were right, while the big-name experts were wrong. Two different companies ran through every last cent of their investors' money. No one who bought stock in either Wicomico Oil or St. Martins Oil struck it rich—or even got their money back. Here's hoping some local farm families got to pocket a few bits of income from those leases they signed.

Two major wells were dug. While working on the first,

crews got 600 feet down before hitting a layer of sand con.
that proved impassable. When the second well got down to 1,000
feet, there was a brief moment of elation when a dark liquid appeared. But then the workmen kept digging and digging, all the
way down to 1,900 feet. No further sign of progress came gush-
ing to the surface.

The Delmarva Oil Craze was over.

There is one entertaining bit of oral history to share before
wrapping this story up. In an old photo I came across in a book
from the "Postcard History Series" titled *Wicomico County and
Delmar*, Wicomico Oil executives have gathered to celebrate a
rare happy moment in the company's history—they were opening a gas pipeline that would provide power to homes in the main
part of Parsonsburg. Those happy days didn't last long, according
to the book's author, John E. Jacob:

*The story is that one Sunday the people returned from
church to find their kitchens flooded. Water was coming through
the gas pipes.*

The last of the true believers was St. Martins Oil and Gas,
a Baltimore company that bought out Wicomico Oil and kept on
digging. In 1923, St. Martins landed in bankruptcy court. The
Wilmington Evening Journal took note of that filing:

*The action recalls the oil boom in Wicomico County in
1913, which created interest in all sections of this country and
drew scores of realtors, representatives of financial interests, ge-
ologists, promoters, prospectors, and many others to the county.*

Here is the *Wilmington Morning News*:

*Although the last derrick has been dismantled and the
county has long since devoted impartial attention to the acquisi-
tion of substantial wealth by the cultivation and development
of the soil, the oil boom of 1913 will remain in the memory [of*

everyone who lived through it].

Postscript: Certificate of Merit

If you are a collector of such things, you can find stock certificates from Wicomico Oil & Gas here and there from online shops that cater to collectors. Do you remember how that stock had a price tag of $1 back when so many oil-world experts regarded the Parsonsburg project as full of hope and promise? Well, one of the certificates that I came across online was priced as a keepsake at $49.95. Adjusting backward for inflation, the certificate is worth roughly $1.75 in 1914 dollars. Hey, that's a return of 75 percent!

THE GREATEST TRIP YOU'LL NEVER TAKE: COBB ISLAND, 1860S

The 1860s were turbulent times in America. Think Civil War, emancipation, presidential assassination, and prolonged recession. The Reconstruction politics of the postwar years were so highly charged that they put our modern-day partisanship to shame.

Under those circumstances, who wouldn't want to get away to a remote barrier island off the coast of Virginia's Eastern Shore? The notion of taking restorative retreats into nature's beauty grew in popularity during these years. Plus, steamboats and railroads put formerly distant locales within reach of hunters, anglers, and beach lovers. More hotels and hunting camps started springing up on islands where the prime business had previously involved serving as cheap places to let animals graze without worrying about whether they'd run off.

In a 1908 book, *The Huntsman in the South*, outdoorsman Alexander Hunter wrote an essay recalling his visit fortysome years before that to a newly opened hotel on Cobb Island. The island takes its name from the family that owned it at that point. The Cobbs were a famously idiosyncratic bunch. In their earliest days as hoteliers, they had no idea what they were doing. But as we'll see, their high-society guests ended up enthralled by the sheer strangeness of the Cobb Island experience.

Fast forward 30 years. When the Cobb Island Hotel was destroyed in an 1890s storm, newspapers all over the country lamented the loss of a resort that ranked among the most famous in the whole country. Cobb Island had come a long way during those three decades.

In the Beginning: Hospitality, Eastern Shore Style

Nathan F. Cobb began life as a New Englander, with family roots there dating back to 1632. Nathan's father fought in the Revolutionary War. The family trades were shipbuilding, fishing, and whaling.

On Christmas Day in 1820, Nathan married the former Nancy Doane. They might have lived happily ever after in New England if Nancy hadn't developed health problems. In the mid-1830s, doctors told Nathan the family should move to a place with milder winters, so he sold his share of the family business interests and sailed south. At least two children were aboard. It's unclear whether their third and youngest son was born before or after the move.

It's also unclear whether the Cobbs had a final destination in mind when they set sail. What we know is that when their ship ran into bad weather, they sought refuge in the little town of Oyster on the lower end of Virginia's Eastern Shore. The townspeople there were so friendly and helpful that the Cobbs decided to stop sailing and make a home in Oyster.

Nathan opened a store. But he soon got to missing the

maritime life. In 1839 he bought an offshore barrier island with $100 worth of gold and a wagonload of a then-precious commodity, salt. He had his mainland home dismantled, then shipped it in pieces out to the island, where he put it back together.

He and his sons went into business as "wreckers," salvaging cargo aboard ships that wrecked in treacherous nearby waters. The Cobbs rescued stranded sailors, too, though they never charged a penny for that aspect of their services. They made money by taking a percentage of the salvaged cargo. That business started to go south when the U.S. government's Life-Saving Service expanded into the area, taking over responsibility for wrecks.

Here is from that essay by Alexander Hunter:

[F]ortune smiled upon them [in the 'wrecking business]. A ship loaded with coffee from Brazil went ashore, and the Cobbs saved the cargo and received $10,000. Another ship panned out $5,000 for salvage, and their last windfall was a three-masted bark of $4,000. ... Then the United States Government built a [life-saving] station, ... and the Cobbs found their salvage fees gone. They had more money than they could spend, but when is man ever content?

The 'Wreckers' Turn to Tourism

The Cobb family grew in numbers through these years. Nathan's three sons came of age, got married, and started having families. Nathan's sickly wife died shortly after the move to Cobb Island. He soon remarried, but the former Esther Carpenter would also fall ill in time, leaving Nathan a two-time widower.

The Cobbs came up with a couple of side gigs to augment their salvage income. Both businesses were built on the natural abundance of their island. Here, again, is Hunter's essay:

You Wouldn't Believe!

This place was then by far the finest shooting grounds on the Atlantic coast for wildfowl and bay-birds. It was not only the feeding-grounds of enormous numbers of brant, geese, and snipe, but, being so far out in the ocean, it attracted, as a resting-place, vast flocks of migrating birds, and it was literally the paradise of sportsmen.

The first side gig was "market" hunting, which involved killing ducks in massive numbers for sale to mainland businesses that in turn supplied the meat to restaurants and stores. The Cobbs also started charging fees to visiting sportsmen who wanted to use their island as a base for hunting and fishing. After their salvage business went south, the Cobbs decided to dive headfirst into this tourism game.

First step: Build a hotel. Alexander Hunter was among the 200 or so guests who booked stays on Cobb Island in the resort's first official season.

I happened to be there at the opening, and it made a greater impression upon me than any seaside resort I ever visited. The attempt of [these] simple-minded, honest fishermen to run a watering-place, without the remotest idea of anything outside of their storm-tossed isle, was certainly unique and rare.

'If They Didn't Like It, They Could Lump It.'

The Cobbs had now come full circle. Drawn to the Eastern Shore by the hospitality of its people, they now became the ambassadors who welcomed outsiders. The elder Nathan wasn't really involved at this point—the hotel was more a project of his sons.

• *Warren Cobb, the eldest son, was a rough and ready mariner, with a voice like a foghorn, and an insatiate thirst. He was a typical ruddy-faced, good-natured, weather-beaten, ocean fisherman. He never refused an invitation to "splice the main-*

brace," and each succeeding drink only made him happier than the one before.

Side note: That phrase, "splice the mainbrace," originally referred to an especially difficult repair job on old sailing ships. Captains used to reward sailors who completed it successfully with a celebratory bit of alcohol, which is how the phrase morphed into a euphemism for drinking.

• *Nathan, the second son, was a very tall, angular man, of powerful build, and withal as gentle and tender as a child. He was the only sportsman in the family, and was, without exception, the finest shot I ever met. He probably killed more wildfowl for market than any other gunner in America.*

• *Albert, the youngest, was the bright one of the family; he was a sport, too, but his game was draw poker.*

The hotel operation hit some bumps in the road early on. The Cobbs hired a "friend of the family" to serve as a clerk, only to watch him do a lousy job and then skedaddle. Also, it took the rough-hewn Cobbs some time to get to know their clientele. Here is a long bit from that Hunter essay, recounting the way things operated during that opening season:

It was truly ludicrous, these untutored, unimaginative wreckers catering to the wants of the delicate, refined pleasure-seekers. Well, the balance was about even; these Norsemen did not understand their guests, and the guests certainly did not comprehend their landlords.

The guests were, for the most part, fashionable people. When the hotel and cottages were filled at the opening of the season the Cobbs were simply dumbfounded that there were people in the world who could want so much. Livery, telegrams, drainage, laundries, water pipes were as Sanskrit to these simple-minded men, and they were as much out of place as was Chris-

topher Sly in the lord's palace [in Shakespeare's "Taming of the Shrew"].

The fare was plentiful, most profuse; in fact, it was served in wholesale quantities. For example, a guest would call for fish, and a huge sea trout, some two feet long, enough for a whole family on Good Friday, would be placed on the table. Bread—a corn-pone the size of a Belgian curbstone would be handed up. Beef—and a collop that would satisfy a Pawnee Indian would arrive. Soft crabs—six at a time would be brought.

Such things as sauces, pickles, condiments, preserves, were unthought of there—simply because they were unheard of. ... These wreckers, like the old Norsemen, were children of Nature; they ate when they were hungry, drank when thirsty, rose with the dawn, and retired to their rest at the end of the day. So, the rich and fastidious sportsmen brought their wives, sisters, cousins, and aunts to the island on a kind of lark—and they had it.

It must be confessed that some of the sportsmen, for the sake of a practical joke, inveigled their people to Cobb's, and many of the visitors expected to find on the island a modern hotel with gas and electric lights, ... superb bar, wine vaults, tonsorial accommodations, billiard saloon, telegraph facilities, and many other things considered by many the necessaries of life; and when they saw the meager establishment, a few actually returned home, but the majority remained, and many declared it to be the best time of their lives.

There was no conventionality at Cobb's, no grades of social position; everyone was on an equal footing, and as one of the Cobbs was heard to remark, "If they didn't like it, they could lump it."

... [I]n the ballroom, where the 'band' was waving and

weaving a 'voluptuous well,' the proprietors would saunter through the room clad in their usual costumes of an oilcloth hat, Guernsey jacket, canvas breeches, and rubber boots reaching to the hip. But withal, there were no [hoteliers] in America that were as popular, for the Cobbs were so sincere, so true, so democratic that they treated all alike. Whether you were noble or serf, rich or poor, famous or unknown, it was all the same to them; and when the visitors left the island it was with regret at the parting.

The Island Takes Off

Through the 1870s and 1880s, Cobb Island grew steadily more popular as a tourism destination. Lots of guests came from Baltimore and Washington, D.C., but almost every state on the Atlantic Coast appears in the hotel register, along with a good number of more distant locales.

The Cobbs made this unlikely success story work by never shying away from big challenges. For all of Hunter's talk about these "untutored" and "unimaginative" men, the brothers proved quite resourceful when it came to problem-solving. They bought and managed a mainland farm to provide guests with home-grown vegetables and fruits. They learned to raise livestock on the mainland so that the hotel menu might include top-flight beef and pork in addition to fresh-shot waterfowl and fresh-caught seafood. In a third mainland project, they built a tide-powered mill so that they could grind their own grain for flour. They even bought a steamboat to make it easier for guests to get to the island. They named that boat the *NWA Cobb*, with the letters representing Nathan Jr., Warren, and Albert. It's no wonder, then:

For many years Cobb's Island was the most famous resort in America.

Postscript: A Stormy End

Nathan Cobb watched this growth unfold from a distance. He and his third wife, Nancy Richardson, bought a farm on the mainland, a few miles south of Oyster. When he died in 1890 at the ripe old age of 93, he was buried outside the kitchen window of that farmhouse. Six years later, a storm ravaged Cobb's Island, destroying the hotel and all of its outbuildings. The Cobbs tried to rebuild the business, but those efforts never came close to achieving the glories of their heyday in the hospitality game.

THE FUTURO HOUSE AIMS FOR THE STRATOSPHERE

Unless you're a pilot taking off from the tiny Eagle Crest Airport or a worshipper bound for Burton Chapel AME Church, there's no reason to take a westbound turn off Coastal Highway onto Eagle Crest Road. But if you do take that detour a little north of Lewes, Del., your reward will be a flying-saucer sighting.

No, really: The science-fiction-looking saucer that soon appears off to your right is an old-school affair, evoking UFOs as imagined back in the 1950s and 1960s. Think "The Jetsons," "Lost in Space," and "My Favorite Martian."

Starting with the Finnish

The story of how this strange sci-fi contraption landed in Milton, Del. begins across the ocean in Finland. That's where the architect Matti Suuronen was born in 1933. Early in his career, Suuronen got interested in using high-tech plastics as a building material. The first time he employed his favorite fiberglass-reinforced polyester plastic was in building a dome atop a grain silo.

Suuronen is best remembered today for putting that material to use in the so-called "Futuro Homes"—that's the official brand name of Milton's flying saucer. This episode began with an old school-days pal of Suuronen's asking a favor: Would the architect build a really cool ski cabin? That friend had two special requests: First, the cabin should heat up quickly upon returning from the chilly slopes, and second, it should be easy to build, even on hilly terrain.

Suuronen dubbed his first stab at this the "After-Ski" cabin. It was made of 16 pieces of his favorite plastic bolted together into the flying-saucer shape that geometry buffs know as ellipsoidal. You could ship the cabin in pieces and put it together on-site, or you could airlift the fully assembled product in by helicopter.

The cabin was elevated on four legs, each bolted to its own concrete "pier"—those piers were much easier to lay than a full foundation. Thanks to the then-latest innovations in polyurethane insulation, the interior could heat up from minus 20 degrees Fahrenheit to a comfy 60 degrees in just 30 minutes.

The cabin stands 13 feet off the ground. Its entrance would have seemed like magic in an old sci-fi movie, but it works basically like a modern garage door opener: Push the button on a remote, and a stairway descends to the ground. The saucer you then climb up into has a diameter of 26 feet. Squeezed inside: a bedroom, bathroom, kitchen, and dining room. Later on, some models would offer a fireplace option.

When the Futuro Was Now
When that "After Ski" cabin started getting attention, Suuronen decided to turn his flying saucer into a new product available to the public. And for a brief stretch of the late 1960s and early 1970s, it seemed like his Futuro homes might really become the next big thing on the second-home real estate market.

You Wouldn't Believe!

Contracts were signed with factories where the homes could be mass-produced. Regional sales agents signed on to start marketing flying-saucer-style weekend abodes. Prices started at $16,000. The target market was young adults with money to spare and hobbies to pursue—not just skiing, but beach trips and hiking excursions as well.

A man named Joe Hudson served as a Delmarva sales rep, operating under the corporate name of New Dimensions of Delaware. He arranged to showcase a Futuro model on land southwest of Lewes, where the Coastal Club housing development is today. He had high hopes at first, as he explained to the *Cape Gazette* newspaper in 2015:

We had long lines of people wanting to see inside, especially on weekends. Sometimes it was so crowded inside people couldn't move. We had a lot of orders.

But the Futuro house never became a hit. One problem was global in nature. The oil crisis of the early 1970s sent the price of plastics through the roof—tripling almost overnight.

The other problem involved local resistance to an exotic new housing style. In one of the smattering of articles on this topic that appeared in regional newspapers, the mayor of Lewes came out "dead set against" placing "spaceship-type homes" in his municipality. The powers that be in that town followed his lead, classifying Futuros as "mobile homes." That meant the spaceships were only allowed in less desirable locations. (Is there a little irony in the way history buffs today want to protect the Futuro homes that their preservation-minded predecessors rejected as too ugly and radical for their town?)

Hudson tried again, this time in Milton. He promised to build a development that would mix traditional homes with Futuros. He promised that the spaceships in that project would be hidden from public view, set behind trees or more traditional-looking buildings. One story in the *Wilmington News Journal* in 1971 paraphrased Hudson bragging that this would be the first real-estate project in the country to feature a sizable number of Futuros.

Alas, the project fell by the wayside. I have been unable to figure out exactly why things went wrong. Perhaps it was those oil-crisis-fueled pricing problems. In Delaware, as in the rest of the country, the Futuro's moment soon passed, though not before at least three of the flying saucers went up in the state.

One was located near Broadkill Beach—that one was torn down, reportedly for scrap. But two survivors are still standing as of this writing. One is in Houston, a small town between Harrington and Milford. It's still there, at 4388 Deep Grass Lane. The third is in Milton on the aforementioned Eagle Crest Road.

Postscript: Of Nude Photos and Cremora Commercials
I can't close this episode without sharing a couple of fun Futuro tidbits. According to Hudson, the Broadkill Beach Futuro was once the site of a risqué nude photo shoot. Hudson also reported that one of his Futuros found its way to Washington, D.C., where it was featured in a TV commercial for Cremora, in which the futuristic hatch opened upon a scene of space-suit clad actors using the powdered coffee creamer. In New Zealand, a Futuro did brief duty as a bank branch.

Nowadays, according to the Hudson family members quoted in the *Cape Gazette*, "not a week goes by" without some stranger stopping to take a photograph. I was part of that parade of goofballs, and if you do the same, you'll be participating in one of Delmarva's stranger travel traditions.

RIDING LIFE'S ROLLER COASTER IN FRANKLIN CITY

Takabisha ranks among the world's steepest, scariest roller coaster rides. Located at the Fuji-Q Highland theme park west of Tokyo, this daredevil affair begins by lifting passengers up to a height of 141 feet, then dropping them at a mind-bending angle of 121 degrees, accelerating to 62 miles per hour in two seconds. If you keep your scaredy-cat eyes open, you'll get fabulous views of Mount Fuji.

Life is full of roller coasterish ups and downs, isn't it? That's as true for towns as it is for people. Consider Franklin City, Virginia—the Takabisha of Delmarva. Its story unfolds in a three-part run of climbing up high and crashing down hard. If you haven't heard of Franklin City, that's understandable. The town's boom-and-bust ride ended in the 1960s courtesy of a dreadful nor'easter history buffs know as the Ash Wednesday storm. The town exists today only in family legends, old photos, and historical writings, but its story still speaks volumes about the economic ups and downs that have long been a part of life in Delmarva communities.

Rising from the Marshland
Like at Takabisha, Franklin City's first rise up the roller-coaster was a dramatic affair. The town emerged at the northern shore of Chincoteague Bay, on a run of marshland in the northeastern edge of Virginia's Eastern Shore. That land was inhospitable and mostly worthless until April 7, 1876. That's when the railroad arrived.

By this point, Chincoteague Bay was already pretty famous for the way its mix of salinity, tides, and other natural attributes created oysters that were especially delectable representatives of the species. Before the railroad, seafood (as well as produce from nearby farms) got shipped to big city markets mostly by way of schooners that were often delayed by slack winds and bad weather. Spoilage was a constant headache.

The reliable railroad cured that headache, setting off a burst of entrepreneurial activity that fueled Franklin City's initial rise. The train station took its name from a former landowner, Judge John Rankin Franklin. A post office appeared. Then came one wharf. Then another. Warehouses went up. Banks opened.

The town's entrepreneurs needed houses to live in. So did their workers. A hotel came along too, catering to businessmen and tourists eager to visit storied Chincoteague Island, five miles away at the other end of Chincoteague Bay. No causeway connected that island to the mainland in those days, so tourists rode the reliable rails to Franklin City, where they hopped aboard a ferry.

'A Perfect Pandemonium'
After six short years, Franklin City grew big enough to try and throw a blow-out Independence Day bash. Nearly 3,000 people

showed up. A brass band from Georgetown, Del. played. The speechifying included a dramatic reading of the Declaration of Independence. Alcohol flowed freely, so much that one alarmed attendee telegraphed this message to a big-city newspaper, where it was quickly printed:

A perfect pandemonium reigned in Franklin City from 2 to 8 o'clock. ... Whiskey was sold plentifully, and hard fighting was the order of the day. ... The whole celebration was a miserable farce.

Personal aside: I started out in journalism covering news in small towns, and that experience is why I laughed so hard while reading the roundabout way a local reporter with the *Peninsula Enterprise* addressed this "miserable farce" business. His or her prose is a model of evasiveness in the service of presenting a community in a positive light.

The celebration passed off pleasantly, considering the vast number of persons present, and the inclemency of the weather. ... Owing to [that] inclemency, ... the people were not as comfortably entertained as the committee could have wished, [but] few ... were the least out of humor on account of the circumstances [that] somewhat marred the occasion. ...

T. F. Colburn, Esq., the proprietor of the Franklin City Hotel, did his best to accommodate his guests, ... but [there was] an "unfortuitous" occurrence that happened in the dining room of the hotel, [involving] a splendid supper which had been prepared [for dignitaries] and left on the table in a room where the doors were supposed to be locked.

Translation: The organizers were overwhelmed by the huge crowd. The weather was godawful. Lots of drenched revelers got drunk out of their minds. There wasn't enough food to go around, which is why one ravenous gang of rowdies raided the hotel dining room and devoured that elegant meal set out in a private dining room. I am imagining that last scene as something out of *Animal House.*

'The Most Curious City Ever Seen'
New wharves kept on coming. Two such projects were approved in 1886, another in 1887, and a fourth in 1888. Surprisingly, that last one was undertaken by a woman identified as "Mistress Mary J. Young, of Accomack County, Virginia." The town's population was now about 200. By 1892, annual ticket sails aboard the ferry to Chincoteague Island topped 4,000. Let's pause here for a second to take in the scenery from aboard that ferry, courtesy of a *Baltimore Sun* writer in 1888:

The trip across the bay [from Chincoteague Island to Franklin City] at such an early hour is not without interest, for it is then when the fishermen's boats are seen spreading sail and darting from the shores to the fishing grounds. Fleets scamper and scud before the stiff easterly breeze and soon leave our steamer in their wake. Then some ... are returning with their boat bottoms covered with delicious trout, fat backs, and many other varieties of the fish family.

Lots of travelers back then took note of Franklin City's idiosyncrasies. A writer for the *Pittsburgh Dispatch* dubbed it "the most curious city ever seen," as "every house stands on piles ... three to four feet above the surface." The *New York Sun* described it as a "queer little community, ... one of the oddest to be found anywhere, ... a city set on stilts."

That 1890 *New York Sun* article painted a wonderfully evocative portrait of the people who lived in that "most curious city:"

The men dress in long-legged rubber boots [and] trilled

cotton overalls and jackets. ...They are all expert boatmen, boat-builders, and sail-makers; they can and do tong, dredge, and cull oysters, to a man. They wear their beards full, and their manners bluff. They never lock their doors at night, because there is not a man there who would steal money.

The women dress in calico, and they wear sun bonnets made of the same low-priced material. They are a handsome lot, however, old and young, calico or not.

To look at the people, men and women, as they go about the streets, a stranger would say that they are a contented lot of laborers working at a dollar a day. ... But let the stranger go into the store of Postmaster Bill Gibbs ... and watch the distribution of the mail. ... A dozen men in their rough clothes are awaiting it, and the letters are passed over the counter as they answer their names. They open the envelopes which have the names of well-known wholesale oyster dealers in New York and Philadelphia printed on the corners, and from half of them out drop checks and statements comforting to look upon.

When the mail has been delivered and the men have hurried away, a talk with Mr. Gibbs shows that for a dozen men who have been there in brown-trilled overalls and long-legged boots, the average income is not far from $7,000 a year.

The historian Bob Jones takes deep dives into local history on a fascinating Facebook page that you can find by searching "Worcester Co., Md. History." He did the math here—that annual salary would approach $200,000 today. Even allowing for exaggeration by the postmaster and/or the reporter, you get the idea: Gobs of money rolled through that Franklin City post office in the early 1890s.

Down in Flames

The Franklin City roller-coaster reached its first crest on May 17, 1896 when, in the early morning hours, a resident named Frank Price awoke from his slumber and peered out the window. A "glare" and "crackling" of light were visible in the nearby rail-road station. This headline soon appeared in the *Peninsula Enterprise*: "Franklin City is in ashes."

Mr. Price raised the alarm. Within minutes, everyone in town was running around screaming "fire." A bucket brigade formed. The town had no fire department. No telegraph lines ran to nearby towns that did have firefighting capabilities.

The wind was blowing stiffly from the southwest, a bad sign. From the *Democratic Messenger* newspaper in nearby Snow Hill, Md.: "People who were not excited so badly as to lose their judgment saw that the town was doomed to destruction."

Twenty-five buildings burned, including the train station and the hotel. Wharves and railroad cars went up in flames. The main roadbed through the town was "warped and torn up for a considerable distance." Many residents "escaped only with their nightclothes on the backs." They "took refuge in boats."

Some businesses had some insurance. Most families did not. The nearby towns of Greenbackville and Stockton responded with compassion and generosity, supplying the "destitute people liberally with food and clothing" during the ordeal of cleaning up.

Second Rise, Second Fall

Franklin City had risen once from nothing. The people figured they could do it again, this time from the ashes. They made quick work of that job. The *Virginian Pilot*, 1900:

Franklin City some two years ago was almost annihilated by fire, but since then its rebuilding has been rapid.

You Wouldn't Believe!

The town grew larger than its pre-fire incarnation—there were more than 100 houses, 15 shucking operations, two hotels, and multiple barrel and canning factories. Years later former resident I.H. Bowen would recall in the *Salisbury Daily Times* newspaper how "salesmen crowded the hotel every night, waiting for the morning boat to Chincoteague [Island]."

In that same article, another longtime resident, Carl Phillips, remembered how two daily freight trains and four daily passenger trains rolled into Franklin City during those boom times. "She was really in bloom!" Phillips marveled.

The crest of this second rise came around the time of World War I when Franklin City's population topped out at 400. The town's second descent started out more slowly than its first, fiery fall, but it ended in a stomach-churning, double-dip of a drop.

The problem started on the other end of the bay, on Chincoteague Island, where businessman J.B. Whealton launched an ambitious project to build an overland link to the mainland. That causeway to Chincoteague opened in 1922, providing a new option for getting the island's oyster, seafood, and farm harvests to the railroad. Simultaneously, as automobiles became more popular, business and leisure travel shifted away from the Franklin City ferry and onto the causeway.

Franklin City found itself mired in slow but sure decline through the 1920s, so the town was already faltering when a hurricane roared through in August 1933. In a 1941 article looking back on those days, the *Richmond Times-Dispatch* says:

Then came [the hurricane], sweeping its business houses into the bay, razing homes until now only about 30 remain. Water did what fire had failed to do, for 35 years earlier the town had been razed by flames and rapidly rebuilt.

You Wouldn't Believe!

Some people gave up on Franklin City, but others set about rebuilding yet again. Unfortunately, a smaller hurricane swept through in 1936. The hotel soon shut down, its wood repurposed to build chicken coops out in the nearby countryside.

Last Dance in Franklin City

By the 1940s, the few newspaper articles that mentioned Franklin City described the place as a mostly uninhabited ghost town. Until recently, I thought that was the end of the story, but I learned otherwise from that Worcester County historian I mentioned, Bob Jones. He introduced me to one last rise-and-fall episode in this story.

In 1949, a New York lawyer and insurance man named Robert Markland chose Franklin City as the place to pursue his entrepreneurial dreams. He tried to make a go of it in the canning business, but that venture faltered after a few years. He and his family then switched gears, opening Markland's Bar & Grill.

Real roadhouse fun with loud music and free-flowing alcohol were hard to find on Virginia's Eastern Shore in those days. Liquor laws were restrictive, and liquor licenses were hard to come by. But the Marklands jumped those hurdles and soon created a hit of a nightspot complete with jukebox, dance floor, and comfort food. Most customers came from the nearby Chincoteague Naval Air Station. In combing through old newspapers, Jones found this gem of a quote from family member John Markland:

Friday and Saturday nights, it was booming. You could put your hand on the building, and it would be shaking.

But this last, raucous rise on the roller coaster didn't last. On orders from President Dwight D. Eisenhower, the Chincoteague Naval Air Station was shut down in the late 1950s. Then, in

1962, the fearsome Ash Wednesday storm wiped out what was left of Delmarva's Takabisha—and the roller-coaster ride came to an end once and for all.

A Neighborly Postscript

Nothing much of Franklin City remains today, but it's still fun to drive down that way and wander through the streets of Greenbackville until you can't go any farther. If the tide is low, you might spy the remains of an old wharf. But there is lots to imagine as you mull over the roller coasterish up and downs of life, including one last tidbit that I came across in a book, *Voices of the Chincoteague*. It's an oral history of life in both Franklin City and Greenbackville.

In the wake of the Ash Wednesday storm, rescue efforts abounded in bigger and more famous places. Helicopters flew out to rescue Chincoteague Islanders. Federal and state aid dollars poured into places like Norfolk and Ocean City. No aid came to Franklin City and Greenbackville. The folks there had only their own resourcefulness—and the generosity of their neighbors. From *Voices of the Chincoteague*:

When those with boats were sure all Greenbackville's citizens were safe from the three days of high tides and gale-force winds, they headed to Franklin City where the water was even higher, to try to rescue the few people still there. Even in the face of great personal risk to themselves, it never occurred to them that they should do anything other than rescue their neighbors.

One man who had a farm outside of town was especially well remembered: [One resident recalled,] "He had a right brand new Massey-Ferguson tractor. He put a farm cart behind that tractor an' he come through all this saltwater with that tractor takin' people out. The tractor was ruined after he'd gone through all this saltwater. But he said he had to help his neighbors—they came first."

Nearly to a person, those interviewed mentioned the fact that "if it had not been for Stockton, I don't know what we'd have done." Stockton ... is [a Maryland town] five miles up the road. ... Tractors with trailers, buses, and whatever they could load people onto took them to Stockton. Some stayed there for up to two weeks until they could clean the mud and silt out of their homes. The Stockton citizens fed them at their firehouse, collected canned goods for later, shared their clothes, and even gave them furniture to rebuild their lives.

WHEN DELAWARE DELIVERED THE 'TRUE SPIRIT OF CHRISTMAS'

When you venture into Southern Delaware during the Christmas season, you are wandering a landscape once known far and wide as the "Land of Holly." That nickname is a distant memory now, but the story behind it is an all-American farmland affair through and through, filled with homespun ingenuity, old-fashioned resourcefulness, and entrepreneurial creativity.

The story of that "Land of Holly" begins in the tiny town of Farmington, near Milford. Just over 100 folks live there today, but its population was triple that in the late 1800s, when it was a bustling place with multiple canneries and fruit-evaporating plants.

Families in Sussex and Kent counties had long engaged in the holiday tradition of gathering twigs from holly trees, with their bright red berries and shiny green leaves, to add a little holiday cheer to their homes. In 1890, Farmingtonian William Buell got the idea of turning that tradition into a side hustle. He harvested wagonloads of those twigs and packed them up into 3,000 crates, each one measuring five feet long and three feet deep. They proved quite popular with big-city customers in New York, Philadelphia, and Chicago, where folks bought them up and spun them into wreaths.

The holly hustle really took off starting in 1898, when a man working for Buell, John T. Watson, suggested shipping ready-to-hang wreaths instead of twigs. This involved having local craftspeople wrap holly branches around switches of pliable sweetgum wood. Buell and Watson tested the idea with a small shipment to a New York seed firm. The next year, they were inundated with orders—according to one account, in the thousands. By 1900 the pair was shipping 5,000 crates filled with finished wreaths as Christmas approached.

Enter the "The Holly Wreath Man"

Buell's neighbors took note of his success. Even small-fry farm families wanted to get in on the act. Mothers and children began crafting holly wreaths in their kitchens. Henry and Eunice Burton ran a general store in downtown Milton, where they decided to let local families trade homemade holly wreaths for staples like eggs and milk. Then they marked up the wreaths and sold them to big-city vendors.

Everything shifted into another gear after the Burtons' daughter, Virginia, fell in love with Charles G. Jones—they were married in 1904. Jones soon set about transforming himself into "The Holly Wreath Man." Virginia had her doubts at first. In fact, she feared her new husband was nuts when he dropped $500 hard-earned dollars on postage for promotional materials hawking natural wreaths from the "Land of Holly."

Charles turned a cool $360 profit in that first year. He was a brilliant marketer. Every crate he shipped was stamped with colorful labels bragging that the contents came "From the Land of Holly." His slogan was, "Quality is Remembered When Price Is Forgotten." Largely because of Jones, Milton earned the nickname of "Hollytown, USA." Local folks soon came up with a name for all the extra train cars that started rolling through town in November and December—"The Holly Express." By this point, the holly-wreath-making industry had spread throughout lower Delaware and moved into Maryland and Virginia as well.

From Seasonal Greens to Real Money

Fast forward to 1936. In the midst of the Great Depression, Southern Delawareans shipped 2 million Christmas wreaths. The way it worked was a kind of prehistoric version of our modern-day gig economy, with scads of different ways for locals to make a buck in the holly trade. Some families transformed farmhouse kitchens into wreath-making stations. Others were solo artists: One woman, Mary Figgs of Millsboro, earned regional renown for her ability to churn out 100 wreaths a day despite a disability—she had only one arm.

Still other families took a more focused approach. They ventured into swamplands full of holly to gather raw materials, then sold those twigs and branches to wreath makers like Mrs. Figgs. On other farms, entire barns were cleared out so that hired hands could work out of makeshift wreath-making factories. Every store around carried wreath-making wire, the only non-natural store-bought ingredient in Delaware's holly wreaths. It was nearly as thin as sewing thread.

The *Wilmington News Journal*, Nov. 27, 1934: *Hundreds of farmers and their wives and children are taking to the woods this week, gathering holly branches from which to make wreaths for window decorations in the city homes and department stores in New York, Philadelphia, Chicago, Boston, Baltimore, and other places. ... During the day the farmer and his boys go into the wood and cut the branches from the trees and carry them home to the womenfolk, who make them into beautiful window decorations.*

In a 2019 *Delaware Wave* article on this topic, the historian Mike Morgan shared these three tidbits from the *Delaware Coast News* on Dec. 7, 1929:

• *One could see automobiles going north with holly in bulk and wreaths piled high on the back seat. ...*

• *Sometimes when so many of the farmer's crops have been a failure, instead of giving up in despair, he plods along slowly, looking forward to the holly season to pull him out of his financial troubles. ...*

• *Excuses are sent to the schools that the children are needed to help with the wreath-making.*

Good Times, Bad Times

Like in any business, there were good years and bad ones. Years with early frosts brought supply-side problems, as berries could be quite hard to find. Other years saw demand-side problems linked to the economic ups and downs in big cities.

Another problem arose courtesy of newcomers to the business who didn't know what they were doing. They would cut branches in the wrong spot and in the wrong way, hindering the regrowth of new twigs in succeeding years. The state's forestry office got in on the act, doling out instructions and pleading with people to cut smaller branches, not larger ones. Sloppy harvesting, those experts warned, could put at risk "the green forest goose that lays the golden Christmas egg."

You Wouldn't Believe!

In 1939, Delaware state legislators passed a law declaring the holly the state's official tree. No wonder: The U.S. Department of Agriculture around that time estimated that some 15,000 people were engaged in the holly trade, earning a combined $450,000. A single family, working hard for weeks on end, could pick up $500 or more in "Christmas money."

Charles G. Jones died in 1944. But his son W.T. Jones stepped right into his late father's marketing-maven shoes. In 1951 the younger Jones made the world's largest-ever holly wreath. It had a diameter of 11.5 feet. It had to be shipped in pieces and bolted back together when it got to New York City, where it hung to much hullabaloo outside of Radio City Music Hall.

The *Wilmington News Journal*, Dec. 5, 1946: *Sussex farmers again this autumn have been making wreaths, finding it not only a profitable on-the-side pastime but also one that gives them the material satisfaction and pleasure of knowing their handiwork will enhance the Christmas festivity in many homes [all] over the land. With their green leaves speaking of life, of growing things, of man's toil and his harvest; and the red berries—of the fire on the hearth, the lights in the windows, and the warmth in human souls, the wreaths comprise perfect tokens of the holiday most dear to all. Wherever they are hung they denote faith, peace, kindness, and goodwill—the true spirit of Christmas.*

The 'Land of Holly' Becomes a Ghost of Christmas Past

Things started going south for the holly wreath game in the 1950s when quality artificial wreaths came on the market. Some of them were made in Delaware, ironically. Fake wreaths were a hit with big-city department stores and other commercial customers, as they could put them up earlier and let them hang for longer periods without worrying about wilting and spoilage.

103

Other factors played a role in the decline as well. As forest lands were cut to make room for new houses and farm fields, holly trees got harder to find. Changes in the economy gave younger women more and different opportunities in the workplace. Fewer and fewer of them chose to keep up the holly traditions they had learned from their mothers.

Perhaps the final nail in the coffin came in the mid-1950s when the U.S. Department of Labor imposed a new minimum wage of $1 an hour and ruled that it applied even to home-based workers. The one-size-fits-all federal rule wreaked havoc in a gig-economy-style holly game in which farm families had a dozen different ways from Sunday to make a buck. Suddenly, federal bureaucrats proclaimed that there was only one way to make a buck—as an official "employee" who received official "wages" in accord with proper payroll and tax-reporting protocols. In the years that followed, Delaware Senator J. Allen Frear introduced legislation in Congress several times seeking to carve out an exemption from these rules for the Delaware holly-wreath market. It never passed.

Things got so bad that the feds even came after the "Holly Wreath Man" himself, accusing W.T. Jones of failing to pay minimum wage. Jones was eventually vindicated, but between a shutdown of operations for one year and the expensive ordeal of proving his innocence, Jones ended up deep in debt. He closed his holly business. He ran an auto parts store in his later years.

Later, he would recall the year the feds shut him down this way:

[It] was like stopping Santa Claus on Christmas Eve.

By the time Jones died in 1997 at the age of 83, the holly industry was long gone. Back in 1965, a *Salisbury Daily Times* reporter had issued a spot-on prediction:

You Wouldn't Believe!

Like cranberry chains and popcorn balls, the holly wreath may soon join the ghosts of Christmas past.

In an unsigned editorial in 1966, the *Daily Times* celebrated the economic trade-off at the heart of the holly-trade tradition:

Urban folks bought themselves a genuine touch of the country for the Christmas season. The country folks earned extra money with which to buy holiday things, some of them from the city.

The piece finished on this sad note:

Perhaps families are not what they used to be and no longer do enough of them gather in a common effort such as wreath-making. ... It's sad to contemplate the likelihood that as some future holiday season approaches, an Eastern Shore tradition will have passed on.

The legacy of the holly industry does live on, actually, but only in fits and starts Local historical societies have put up exhibits about it. Libraries have brought in guest speakers to reminisce about the good ol' holly days. Senior centers have put on wreath-making sessions to remind residents about their childhood joys. A historic marker in Milton Memorial Park honors "The Holly Industry." Another marker stands in front of the home of the original "Holly Wreath Man," Charles Jones. Also in Milton, there is an annual Holly Festival at Christmastime.

BEACONS!

THE GREATEST HONEYMOON IN HISTORY

When 19-year-old Vernon Cooper landed at the mouth of the Wicomico River, the Wisconsin native didn't catch on immediately that he'd found his forever home. He didn't have a crystal ball. He couldn't see the Dames Quarter gal in his future.

The U.S. Coast Guard stationed Vernon at Great Shoals Light in 1951. That screwpile affair had been guiding vessels on their way to and from Salisbury, Md. since the oyster gold rush days of the 1880s. The beacon stood out in the water at the upper end of Tangier Sound, two miles by boat from the nearest post office—yup, that was in the town of Dames Quarter.

Vernon shared tight quarters in that cottage-style beacon with two other staffers. Their drinking water was collected in barrels set under the roofline of the cottage to collect rainwater. Later, Vernon would recall how grossed out he was at the sight of gulls and other birds doing their business on that roof. There was another reason he wasn't thrilled over his new assignment:

I was lonely and very, very bored. People would come by [in boats], wave, holler to us. That was about it. No visitors.

107

Each lighthouse staffer was responsible for his own meals. Vernon didn't know how to cook. He soon landed in a doctor's office on the mainland, complaining of persistent stomach pains. The doctor asked, "What are you eating?" Vernon's answer involved hot dogs, hamburgers, and, well, that's it.

The days all ran together. Polishing, scrubbing, painting, log-book writing, re-filling the lamp with fuel. No shower, no bathtub. There wasn't even hot water, unless he warmed some up on a ramshackle stove. Doing laundry involved an old-school washboard.

That Dames Quarter Gal

Vernon served shifts that ran 21 straight days. Then he got a week off. Presumably, it was during one of those off-duty stretches that he met 21-year-old Juanita Bozman, though it's also possible that he first laid eyes on her while during one of his on-duty boat trips that involved stops at the post office or supply runs to a store in Dames Quarter that was run by Delmas and Eva Shores.

However the meeting happened, it must have been love at first sight, or very close to it. Vernon and Juanita were married within six short months.

That's where this story takes a fun turn. Lighthouse staffers have a reputation as sticklers for rules and regulations. Surprise visits by supervisors happened now and again—those staffers had to have the beacon ready at all times to pass a rigorous "white-glove" inspection.

But a romantic notion grabbed hold of Vernon's heart and wouldn't let go. Somehow, he convinced his Great Shoals compadres to go along with his scheme. The two other men left the lighthouse so that Vernon and Juanita could have a weeklong honeymoon alone on Great Shoals Light. No one sent official dispatches to higher-ups requesting time off. The other guys simply went AWOL.

The honeymoon suite on Great Shoals was a cramped affair involving twin bunk beds. The powder room was a rickety outdoor privy hanging out over the water.

The *Salisbury Daily Times* did two stories over the decades about this 1951 interlude. Both were written by first-rate chroniclers of Delmarva history and culture—the first, in 1972, by Orlando Wootten, and the second in 2002, by Brice Stump.

Juanita was 72 years old when she was interviewed for that latter story. She had suffered two strokes by this time and was fighting cancer as well. But her description in that interview of those honeymoon days hints at the vibrant personality that flipped Vernon head over heels:

We fished, we swam, listened to the radio and danced–and had sex, lots of sex.

In between romantic interludes, Juanita went to work. She took over the cooking duties. She helped Vernon refill that lamp. Perhaps it came naturally to her because her grandfather, Calvin Bozman, had been a keeper at the not-so-far-way Hooper Strait Lighthouse. (Alas, that assignment ended in tragedy. In September 1918, a passing ship reported that the lighthouse was dark. An oyster boat soon came upon Bozman's body, drifting in the strait. An investigation concluded that he had fallen from a storage platform while sawing wood.)

For Vernon, that honeymoon transformed the loneliness of life on a lighthouse into something approaching heaven on earth. In Juanita's memories, everything about that week in the summer of 1951 was perfect. Here is what she told Orlando Wootten:

There never was more perfect weather. The sun shone all day, and the moon at night. We had the whole place to ourselves with not a neighbor for miles, except for passing boats.

Forever Home in Somerset County

The cottage-style beacon at Great Shoals continued to light the way into the Wicomico River well into the 1960s. But then its light was automated, and the Coopers' honeymoon cottage was torn down. Its metal foundation remains in place today, support-ing a light that shines from a pole. Lots of older locals still miss the romance of that old-school cottage.

Juanita and Vernon never got a chance to go back and pay a visit. Juanita was sad to hear that their honeymoon cottage had disappeared from the Wicomico.

I really loved that old lighthouse, and just hated to see it torn down. We spent a wonderful week there, and no one ever found out.

During his 20 years with the Coast Guard, Vernon was stationed on the other side of the Chesapeake Bay at Solomons Island for a while. He also did time in the Aleutian Islands of Alaska and in Chicago. Juanita followed him on those travels, of course. When their wandering years came to an end, the couple returned to Somerset County.

Vernon owned the Anderson Marine hardware store on Deal Island. He also held several posts over the years with the state of Maryland. He hung onto one thread of his Wisconsin roots, becoming well known as the biggest Green Bay Packers fan in Somerset County. He hung out with the straight-shooting gang at the Manokin Gun Club as well.

Juanita spent most of her married years in the roles of housewife and mother. She was very active in the American Le-gion Ladies Auxiliary. In their later years, the couple lived in the town of Princess Anne.

You Wouldn't Believe!

Juanita died in 2004 at the age of 76. Vernon joined her on the other side in 2011 at age 81. The couple had five children. At the time of Vernon's death, they had eight grandchildren and five great-grandchildren. Here's hoping the two of them are enjoying an everlasting second honeymoon on a heavenly beacon.

WILD RIDE ON SHARPS ISLAND LIGHTHOUSE

Many of you have climbed up into the cottage of a screwpile lighthouse. Perhaps in St. Michaels, Md. at the Chesapeake Bay Maritime Museum. Or in Cambridge, Md. on the Choptank River waterfront. Perhaps you were in a beacon on a windy, cold day— if so, did you feel the cottage shaking?

OK, now imagine three things:

(1) You're in a cottage that stands out in the middle of the water, far from land.

(2) A deep winter freeze is lifting. The run of ice that stretched out to your cottage is melting, breaking into humongous chunks that ride the waves.

(3) It's so foggy you can't see a thing.

OK, imagine more things:

(4) The wind kicks up. A storm rolls in. Those waves get high and wild.

(5) Those giant chunks of ice are still riding those waves. Every thwack against the legs of the lighthouse sends a shudder through the structure.

(6) BAM! Your legs come out from under you, and you're tumbling wildly. You come to rest against a wall. Or is it the ceiling? You don't even know that much in this frantic moment. You scan your body: *Am I bleeding? Am I hurt?*

Your mind is frantic: *What just happened?* You piece it together: The cottage got thrown off of its metal foundation. It's now down in the frozen, churning water, riding those wild waves—and you are still aboard.

This actually happened to keeper Christopher Columbus Butler and assistant Charles L. Tarr at the Sharps Island Lighthouse on the morning of Feb. 10, 1881. Spoiler alert: Who knew those cottages atop screwpile lighthouses could float?

This Lighthouse Locale Was Jinxed

Sharps Island never had any luck with lighthouses. In days gone by, the island rose from the Chesapeake Bay at the mouth of the Choptank River, a little way below Tilghman Island, Md. That location may ring a bell if you've read the novel *Chesapeake* by James Michener, as it's roughly where Michener placed the fictional Devon Island. Fictional Devon and real-world Sharps shared the same fate at the end of their respective stories—they sunk under the Bay and disappeared forever.

No one knows for sure how big Sharps Island might have been during the centuries when Choptank Indians rowed out there to fish and hunt. Historians guesstimate that it covered 700 acres during the 1600s. That's when it got its name by virtue of being owned by a Quaker doctor named Peter Sharpe.

The island was down to 400-and-some acres in the mid-1800s. By 1900, it covered less than 100 acres. By 1960, it was gone. There is talk in old newspaper articles about how some homes on Tilghman Island and some decoys crafted by local carvers were made with wood liberated by scavenging locals who dismantled structures like the doomed Sharps Island Hotel.

About those bad-luck beacons. The first Sharps Island Lighthouse was built on land in 1838. Folks understood back then that the island was disappearing, but they underestimated how quickly that process was happening. Just 27 years later, the U.S. Light House Board gave up on that structure, citing "the gradual washing away of the ground."

The following year, 1866, a screwpile lighthouse went up out in the middle of the water. Like its predecessor, it marked the entrance to the Choptank. Folks also understood back then that screwpile lighthouses might be vulnerable to ice floes in stormy weather. But that style of lighthouse was easy to build compared with the sturdier caisson-style lighthouses. Caissons still ranked new-fangled things. Plus, they were more expensive to build.

So the lighthouse powers that be went with the tried-and-true screwpile. A spot of trouble arose in the winter of 1879 when two diagonal braces went flying off the lighthouse, thanks to storm-driven ice floes. That same winter saw ice-related damage to another brace and a horizontal beam. Everything was repaired. Out of an abundance of caution, an ice-breaking pile of rocks was installed south of the beacon.

Ridin' the Storm Out
Another deep freeze arrived in 1881. The ice had started to thaw by the morning of Feb. 10. Fog rolled in, followed by a storm. This time, the wave-riding ice floes knocked Sharps Island Light-house completely off of its foundation. Incredibly, keeper Butler and assistant Tarr did not suffer serious injuries in the tumble.

But they now found themselves inside a floating cottage. Incredibly, that structure did not seem to be in imminent danger of sinking. And so the keepers rode the storm out. For 16 long hours, the cottage floated with the waves. Finally, at 1 a.m. the next morning, they ran aground off the west end of Tilghman Island, at Paw Paw Cove.

Their wave-tossed ride had covered five meandering miles.

In the hours that followed, keepers Butler and Tarr provided ample justification for the historical reputation that lighthouse keepers have for a fanatical devotion to duty. The lifeboat known as a dory was still attached to the cottage. The pair could have rowed ashore at any time. Instead, here is what the writer Pat Vojtech reports in her book *Lighting the Bay: Tales of Chesapeake Lighthouses:*

The two keepers were shaken, cold, wet, hungry, and exhausted, yet they stood by the wrecked lighthouse through the night hours, waiting for a passing vessel that might help them salvage the lighthouse property. When fog moved in, obscuring [their view of potential] passing vessels, they finally gave up and paddled their way to shore in the lighthouse dory.

Butler and Tarr took a brief break on land, then returned to the cottage to retrieve the most valuable items–the lens, its pedestal, fuel oil, logbooks, etc. They even took empty oil cans back with them. For obvious reasons, inspector F.J. Higginson of the U.S. Lighthouse Service recommended that Butler and Tarr be awarded letters of commendation.

The keeper and assistant clung to the fallen house ... for sixteen and half hours. Their danger was very great, being in the midst of heavy flowing ice, which would often pile upon on the house and thereafter swamp it.

Third Time, *Not* the Charm

A few hours after Butler and Tarr rescued those valuables, the Sharps Island lighthouse slid off its shallow, temporary resting place in Paw Paw Cove and headed back out to sea. A couple of days after that, a steamboat ran aground on Sharps Island, possibly because that lighthouse was missing. Thankfully, there were no serious injuries or deaths.

A new lighthouse went up at Sharps Island the next year, 1882. This time, the Light House Board wisely went with one of those sturdy, newfangled caisson-style beacons. The iron tower was 37 feet tall. Its concrete-filled caisson foundation was 30 feet deep and 30 feet in diameter.

For 95 years, that lighthouse stood up to everything Mother Nature could throw at it, including ice. Then came the incredible deep freeze of 1976-77. Sharps Island Lighthouse emerged from all the expanding and contracting and melting and thwacking of those icy months as "The Leaning Tower of the Chesapeake."

It still stands that way out there today, askew by about 20 degrees. It is, Pat Vojtech says in her book, the only caisson on the Chesapeake Bay ever damaged in this way by ice. Sharps Island never did have any luck with lighthouses.

ALL ALONE AT
CHERRYSTONE BAR

Lighthouses fire up the imagination, don't they? For some people, the beacons of the Chesapeake and Delaware bays evoke the romantic days of sail, a parade of ships from days gone by—schooners, pungies, bugeyes, skipjacks, and steamboats.

For others, nature is center stage. These folks imagine themselves perched on the deck before a sunrise flush with drama, a majestic flock of waterfowl moving across the horizon.

Still others cheer the bravery of first responders. So many lighthouse keepers performed so many heroic deeds over the centuries while responding to wrecks and collisions.

Then there is Oscar Daniels. In 1909 he worked as a keeper on the Cherrystone Bar Lighthouse, a cottage-style beacon that helped vessels make their way into the harbor at Cape Charles, Va. between 1858 and 1918.

Daniels saw his share of bugeyes, skipjacks, and steamboats out there. He admired his share of sunrises and sunsets. But none of that consoled him on the day in 1909 when he sat down to write in the Cherrystone Bar logbook:

117

A man has just as well die and be done with the world at once as to spend his days here.

He signed this entry, "All Alone."

Keepers often had assistants. But sometimes they didn't. And other times those assistants had time off. Long days passed in complete isolation from their fellow humans. On a winter day in 1916, Mrs. M.F. Edgar was sailing on the Choptank River near Oxford, Md. She spied a large "matchbox" bobbing with the waves and fished it out. Inside was a note from Choptank River Lighthouse keeper John E. Faulkner:

This note was thrown from the Light House in the hope that the finder is enjoying good health and wishing a happy new year to the finder. I am alone today. My assistant has gone ashore to see his family.

So go ahead, put those old sailing ships and glorious sunsets in your mind's eye when you next admire a lighthouse. But give a thought too, to the loneliness of the lighthouse keeper.

Postscript: Three Lives of the Lighthouse

There is a fun bit of trivia around the two lighthouses mentioned here, Cherrystone Bar and Choptank River. The Virginia lighthouse was deactivated in 1919 after improvements were made to the harbor at Cape Charles. The cottage was 61 years old at that point, but still in great shape. The Coast Guard hoisted that cottage onto a barge and then moved it into a warehouse on land.

Two years later it was loaded onto another barge for a sixtysome-mile journey up to Maryland, where the first Choptank River Lighthouse had been destroyed by ice. The Cherrystone Bar cottage then served for another fiftysome years as the second Choptank River Lighthouse. Trivia time: It's the only lighthouse on the Chesapeake Bay to serve in two different states.

You Wouldn't Believe!

The Cherrystone/Choptank cottage was demolished in the 1960s, but it came back to life again in 2012. Community activists in Cambridge used the pre-civil-war construction plans from Cherrystone to build the replica Choptank River Lighthouse that stands today as a tourist attraction on the town's Long Wharf waterfront. As of this writing, it's open daily between May and October.

THE KEEPER WHO LASHED HIMSELF TO HIS BEACON

Delve into a historical topic often enough, and certain words come to serve as red flags. So it is with *lashed*. When that word pops up in stories of shipwrecks from the sailing days of yore, it signals a desperate turn, the story moving from dangerous to deadly.

The turn usually goes like this: The vessel gets caught up on some shoal. Wind and waves start beating that boat into shreds. At some point, the sailors see that it's just a matter of time. So, in a desperate stab at self-preservation, they climb up into the rigging and tie themselves to a mast. All they can do now is wait for a miracle, and that will likely mean spending hours on end above the raging seas, praying and waiting for help to arrive. The lashing will allow them to stay aloft through exhaustion, hypothermia, and unconsciousness.

But that word *lash* leads in a surprising direction in the story that unfolded in Tangier Sound on the evening of April 16, 1910. A fierce gale was blowing, pushing the seas into "mountainous" waves that swamped a sailboat. (None of the reports I've seen identify that boat by name or give a number of crew members.)

A lone man had his eye on the seas that night—Charles A. Sterling, the keeper at Tangier Sound Lighthouse. That beacon stood south of Tangier Island, Va. marking both the southernmost entrance to the sound and a dangerous nearby shoal.

Sterling spied that vessel in distress from his perch on the lighthouse. He noted a broken mast, cracked clean through about 10 feet above the water. Flags of distress flew from that stump.

What could Sterling do? He was alone. He had no radio. There was no way the little lighthouse launch boat would be able to reach that distant vessel in seas this rough.

But like so many other first-responder heroes through the centuries, Sterling couldn't just stand there and watch. Tangier Sound Lighthouse was a screwpile affair, topped by a rectangular cottage. Above the living quarters was a widow's walk that wrapped around the base of the tall glass chamber that housed the beacon. Sterling stepped out onto that walk. He must have used some sort of ladder to climb through wind and rain up the side of that glass chamber. Atop the chamber was a steep-sloped metal roof that must have been slick as all get out.

Sterling's destination was the dome-shaped cupola atop that roof. Somehow, he made it. Once there, he lashed himself to that architectural detail. He had managed to carry a lantern with him. He lay out there in the wind and rain for at least two hours. And for almost every second of that stretch, he waved that lantern back and forth in as wide an arc as his arms could manage.

He hoped that someone out in the darkness might notice something awry with the way the beacon was blinking. Incredibly, it worked. Someone on shore did see that swinging gleam and successfully guessed its meaning. A man identified in later newspaper stories as "Captain Crockett" ventured from his safe harbor into the teeth of the gale. He soon found that sailboat beached on that shoal, where it was still getting beaten to shreds.

Captain Crockett rescued the crew. No one died. Stories about Sterling's selfless, heroic *lashing* appeared in several newspapers around the country.

Postscript: More on That Sterling Character

Sterling did time as a keeper for at least two other Virginia lighthouses. While stationed on Craney Island Light at the mouth of the western shore's Elizabeth River, he received a commendation for his response to the 1927 collision of the steamship *Gratitude* and a scow. The crash happened about 500 yards from the lighthouse. Sterling responded by ringing the lighthouse bell at a furious pace, which drew the attention of another steamboat, the *Pennsylvania*. That vessel soon rescued 268 of the boat's 280 passengers. The other 12 passengers had jumped overboard—Sterling rescued them in his little launch boat.

Sterling also did a stint at Hog Island Light on the Virginia barrier island of that name. While stationed there, he published a 40-page pamphlet detailing the glories of that island's natural and cultural bounty. Here is one excerpt about the religious life of Hog Islanders:

There are two hundred and fifty inhabitants. It is an intensely religious community; they believe in a personal God and a personal Devil, with all the adjuncts of fire, sulfur, and brimstone. ... To be born, reared, live, and die on Hog Island would seem to insure free passport to Heaven; that is, if the keeping of all the Commandments means redemption.

The native Hog Islander is baptized early and is orthodox to a painful degree. He honors his father and mother as much

*as a desert Bedouin; he keeps Sunday with the fidelity of an old
Scotch Covenanter. He does not curse, kill, or steal, and as for
making love to his neighbor's wife, the idea never enters his
head; at least there is no record of this latest American fashion
being practiced in the [Hog Island] Commonwealth.*

*... These islanders are not perfect beings with angel wings
sprouting between their shoulders; their great shortcoming is the
human failing of envy mixed with some uncharitableness. They
gossip about each other, but there ... is no malice in their words,
no desire to injure each other. They are brought up in an atmosphere too pure for that; the seamy side of life never meets their
eyes, and poverty and crime are unknown.*

*... The natives of this island are a fascinating study. ...
They are the result of the evolution of nearly two hundred years
and show that when a community lives a temperate, chaste life,
nature rewards them royally by giving them long life and perfect
content.*

On the Rocks at Cape Henlopen

NOTE: My other books include lots of wondrous tales from days gone by. This excerpt from Eastern Shore Road Trips #1: 27 One-Day Adventures on Delmarva *is one section in an excursion to Rehoboth Beach and surroundings.*

Sometimes the best stories a pretty scene has to tell are actually hiding in the shadows. Consider the majestic Delaware Breakwater East End Light, which stands off a sliver-of-moon-shaped stretch of beach at Cape Henlopen State Park in Lewes. The stately beacon has five levels— entrance, kitchen, bathroom, sleeping quarters, and watch room. The light up top shines from 61 feet above sea level.

She was built in 1885, but the story I want to focus on here goes back quite a bit further. As you'll see while standing on the beach, Delaware Breakwater East End stands near the end of a long run of giant, shadowy rocks. Those rocks are known as the Delaware Breakwater, which ranks as one of the first big public works projects in U.S. history.

You Wouldn't Believe!

Johns Quincy Adams was our sixth president, but he was the first to really try and get the federal government involved in improving the transportation infrastructure of the still-young country. Previous presidents had seen that as an issue for the states. When Adams looked around for important projects to take on, Cape Henlopen landed near the top of his priority list.

Located along a key trade route into Philadelphia, the cape was a dangerous place. Lots of vessels got caught up on tricky, ever-shifting shoals here. To make matters worse, no shelter from storms could be found anywhere around. Nearly 200 ships were wrecked or disabled hereabouts between 1807 and 1826.

By the time Adams got elected, merchants and sailors were begging for something to be done. The project that Adams embraced ranked as an engineering marvel in those days—this was the first breakwater ever built in the Western Hemisphere and just the third in the world, after one in France and another in England.

The designer of the project was Philadelphia architect William Strickland, who is often credited in history books with helping to launch the Greek Revival style in America. He also designed an earlier, long-gone lighthouse that was located near where Delaware Breakwater East End stands today.

Construction of the breakwater began in 1828. Do you know how modern-day infrastructure projects seem to drag on and on, causing highway delays and lane closures for years? Consider yourself lucky: Work on the breakwater stretched on for four-plus decades, lasting clear into the 1870s. More than 800,000 tons of stone were dumped into the water to create a main 2,100-foot-long breakwater and a separate 1,700-foot-long "icebreaker."

The line of rocks rising above the surface here at the

beach is about 20 feet wide. The foundation of rocks at the bottom of the bay is 145 feet wide.

The project took so long to complete that it was basically obsolete on the day it opened. The problem was size—shipping traffic had grown by leaps and bounds during those construction decades, so much so that as many as 200 ships would try and crowd into the fancy new breakwater during bad weather. Still other ships were stuck outside, unable to squeeze into the safe zone. Several ships got wrecked in an 1877 hurricane.

The first effort to try and fix this involved closing the gap between the breakwater and the icebreaker to make the safe zone a little bigger. A second, lasting solution came in the 1920s with the completion of an outer breakwater called the Harbor of Refuge that's more than twice as long as the original inner one. A second lighthouse, also called the Harbor of Refuge, stands out there as well. That addition stretched the size of safe harbor available to more than 1,000 acres.

Considering how many ships, lives, and dollars they saved, the two breakwaters have earned their shared spot in the National Register of Historic Places. Apparently, the only people left out in the cold were, according to one historical account, "the hardy souls who make their living from salvaging wrecks and the 'anchor sweepers' who swept the bay bottom in search of ... scrap iron." These ghoulish operations went out of business after the revamped breakwater made things safer.

You Wouldn't Believe!

CRIME!

Charlestown's Innocent Stream with a Deadly Name

The last time I was in Charlestown, on Maryland's Upper Eastern Shore, I didn't pay the slightest attention to a little spit of water called Peddler's Run. There were lots of better-known things to gawk at in this history-laden piece of Cecil County—the gorgeous waterfront on the North East River, a bevy of interesting colonial-era buildings, and the various signs summarizing stories from days gone by. Charlestown had some brushes with greatness back in its heyday–Benjamin Franklin and George Washington spent time here during their travels.

But I wish I'd known to look for that itty-bitty stream. Its presence speaks to what life was like on the Delmarva Peninsula in colonial times. Think romantic dates, old-time fiddling, drunken benders, an unspeakable crime, and, perhaps, a headless ghost.

A Colonial Fair for the Ages

As historic towns go, Charlestown is like a comet—its time in the limelight was brief but brilliant. The folks who started the town in the 1740s were supremely confident that it would soon surpass

Baltimore as the metropolis of the Upper Chesapeake Bay. Things got off to a promising start, actually. One reason for that was the success of the Charlestown Fair.

First held in May 1744, the fair was a colonial version of our modern downtown block parties. They shut down the streets for a mix of entertainment and commerce that drew patrons from near and far. In some years, Charlestown hosted multiple fairs, with events in April, May, and October.

Merchants came from Baltimore, Philadelphia, and many other towns, setting up shop on the town square in "rude structures made of bushes" that measured 10 feet by 10 feet. Interestingly, that's the same footprint made available to vendors at many Delmarva events nowadays. The rental fee was seven shillings and sixpence.

Festivalgoers, too, came from all over, arriving by boat or on horseback or aboard Conestoga wagons. Here is historian George Johnston, writing in 1881:

[They] came from distant parts of Chester and Lancaster counties [in Pennsylvania] ... to see the sights and have a frolic, and sometimes to settle the feuds and quarrels that had existed in the neighborhood where they lived. ... [There was] fiddling and dancing, as well as frolicking and fighting.

The fairs were especially popular with Irish immigrants, Johnston says:

They had walked barefoot many weary miles, ... for it was customary [in their native land] for the females who traveled to [such a] fair on foot to carry their shoes and stockings in their hands, and when they arrived at the outskirts of town to wash their feet in a convenient stream, after which they put on their shoes and stockings and entered the town.

Quite a few of those lasses probably washed their feet in Peddler's Run.

Fishermen, too, flocked to the fairs, especially when the events coincided with the close of "fisher," or the end of the fishing season on the Susquehanna and other nearby rivers. In 1807, to cite just one year at random, 16,000 barrels of shad and herring were cured and packed annually in Cecil County. The *Baltimore Sun* talked about those fishermen in a 1933 article looking back at the history of the fair:

Sober as they were at home, the travelers often partook too freely of the flowing bowl–and at the Charlestown Fair, they became riotous. The fair became a menace.

But the fair was glorious in many other respects. Women shopped for items that were usually available only in big cities. Those Irish couples danced to fiddle music. Vendors at the fair were the ones who introduced the exotic beverages of tea and coffee to locals, selling packets complete with printed instructions on preparing those newfangled concoctions. Coffee was much more popular than tea.

The Stream Runs Red

The story of how Peddler's Run got its name is drenched in blood. I have come across two versions, one by the aforementioned historian George Johnston in his book *History of Cecil County, Maryland* and one by a correspondent writing under the name "Azton" in the *Cecil Whig* newspaper in 1871.

Azton claims to be quoting from a diary-like telling of the incident by another anonymous gentleman who in turn "obtained his information from a reliable source." That source is described as straight "from the lips of an aged man ... who now slumbers in the silent tomb." Azton's tale begins with this scene-setter:

Those who have ever traveled the road from Charlestown to the village of North East must be familiar with a small streamlet that crosses the road about one and a half miles from the former place, and known by the name of Peddler's Run. This little gurgling stream glides smoothly and silently along in its wandering course, unconscious that its crystal waters had ever been crimsoned by the life-blood of the murdered, and here too the wild bird of the forest pauses in his onward flight, alights to cool his fluttering wing therein, little dreaming of the dark crime that hangs around this spot.

The victim of that dark crime was a vendor at the Charlestown Fair, though there is no record of his name. Azton claims that he is buried near the spot where today's Route 267 (Bladen Street) crosses Peddler's Run. He says that a "rude" headstone once marked the spot. The crime occurred during the fair in or around the year 1785. Here is Azton again:

The black-hearted villain who perpetrated this dark deed of a crime, after having stabbed his victim a number of times, dragged his lifeless body into the bushes nearby, and after having robbed him of his purse, and whatever property of value that might be found upon his person, was about to leave his victim to his fate, when his attention was arrested by the clattering of horses' feet.

The killer panicked. Desperate to stay out of sight of the approaching riders, he climbed a nearby tree. The horses came to a stop at the stream. The riders led the animals to the shore, urging them to drink.

But no sooner had they put their noses to the water than they threw them high in the air and gave each a wild snort, and their riders could not prevail upon them to taste of the water of this troubled stream.

The riders started nosing around. Why were the horses spooked?

They had proceeded but a few steps when one of them discovered what appeared to be a drop of blood upon a stone.

There was more blood nearby. That peddler's body turned up. They spotted the murderer hiding in the tree. The two riders took the man into custody. He was later tried, found guilty, and, in Azton's account, "executed on the spot where the murder was committed."

The historian Johnston tried to find an official account of the case in the county records, but came up empty. The only legal remnant of the case is this:

The stream is yet known by the name of Peddler's Run.

Postscript: Ghostly Visions

As the new country took shape in the decades after the Revolutionary War, Charlestown lost its luster as a rising-star town. It was in the running to be named the seat of Cecil County, but lost out to nearby Elkton. Merchants started bypassing Charlestown in favor of towns like Baltimore and Havre de Grace. The fairs that began in the 1740s continued for nearly a century, finally dying out in the late 1820s.

There is one postscript that needs to be added here, however. It comes courtesy of our friend Azton:

Often when a boy, have I listened to the many strange stories told by the superstitious, who have had occasion to pass by this spot after night had set in, of a peddler without head that might often be seen there. Did time permit, I might tell you many

You Wouldn't Believe!

strange things concerning this haunted stream, but perhaps I have already occupied too much of your time and will, for the present, close.

I am thinking that when I finally do go looking for Peddler's Run, I will do so during daylight hours.

THE LABOR DAY RIOT IN OCEAN CITY

The incident that set off the Labor Day Riot in Ocean City, Md. began as a trifling affair. On the Saturday evening of Sept. 4, 1960, the owner of a boardwalk arcade got into a little spat with a young man from Baltimore. The owner thought that the young man was crossing the line that separates teenage fun from delinquency.

I came across two versions of this argument in old newspaper articles. In one, the young man turned up the volume on the arcade jukebox over and over again. In the other, he insisted on riding atop a hobby horse meant for children. Neither is a big crime, but either could be quite an aggravation for a small business owner dealing with holiday-weekend crowds.

That owner, George J. Galkas, eventually told the young man to leave his arcade. The young man refused. Galkas called the police. The patrolman who responded was a part-timer named Joseph Laramore, brought in to help with those holiday-weekend crowds. Laramore lived in Denton, Md. and worked full time as a constable in Caroline County.

This is where a trifling affair turned treacherous. Things quickly went south between Laramore and the young man. What set the Labor Day Riot in motion was Laramore's decision to break out his nightstick and crack it on the head of that young man, whose name was Laren Baker and who was a U.S. marine private first class on leave from Camp LeJeune, N.C.

A Summer of Simmering Anger

The swing of that nightstick did not happen in a vacuum. Several months earlier, as the summer of 1960 began, Ocean City's leaders had decided that it was time to protect their town's reputation as a family-friendly resort. They ordered police to crack down on all manner of teenage offenses, from underage drinking to delinquency. Over the course of three hot months, the tension had been building.

A throng of teenagers hanging out on nearby stretches of boardwalk and beach saw Baker get thwacked with that nightstick. They were outraged. Some tried to intervene on the spot, tussling with Laramore as he and other officers struggled to drag Baker off the boardwalk and into a patrol car.

After that car pulled away with Baker inside, the anger that had been building among young people all summer erupted into rage. They decided to go down to the police department and demand the release of that marine. As they made their way on an 11-block march, word of what had happened spread through Ocean City like wildfire. A crowd of dozens turned into a few hundred and then swelled into a mob of 2,500. The rowdier members of that mob flipped over several parked cars along the way.

'Throwing Bottles, Cans, Even Lawn Furniture'

It was midnight when this furious crowd arrived at the station on

Dorchester Street. Many had armed themselves along the way with bottles, sticks, rocks, and whatever else they could grab. The *Baltimore Evening Sun:*

[A] wild, screaming crowd of young people ... formed a ring around the station house and demanded the release of the marine.

At the first signs of trouble, Mayor Hugh T. Cropper, Jr. had ordered his police officers to stand down and avoid engaging with the angry teens. The mayor explained later to a reporter "that he thought the absence of police would calm the crowd." He was wrong.

Luckily, a bigwig with the state police named William H. Weber just so happened to be vacationing at the beach that weekend. He made an emergency call, and 30 state cops from all over the lower Eastern Shore were soon speeding toward Ocean City. Meanwhile, Mayor Cropper reversed his no-engagement rule and sounded the town's fire sirens, calling in volunteer firefighters as reinforcements for his overwhelmed police officers.

Those firefighters hooked up hoses and sent word across the riot lines to the teenagers that it was time to disperse. The teens were having none of it. Firefighters turned the hoses on. In return, as the *Evening Sun* put it:

The more violent persons in the crowd rushed forward in waves to throw bottles, cans, stones, and even lawn furniture taken from nearby homes at the firefighters and policemen.

The battle lasted for four hours. Incredibly, no one was seriously injured. Finally, about 4 a.m., the crowd dwindled down to nothing, and calm returned to the streets of Ocean City. The streets now looked like a war zone, however, with "broken bottles and smashed furniture, littering the streets, sidewalks, and lawns."

The Aftermath of the Riot

Thirty-three young people were arrested that night. Almost all got charged with disorderly conduct. One newspaper said the city jail was so overcrowded that 16 teens spent the night in a cell that had just three cots. The arrestees hailed from all over—Baltimore and its suburbs; Washington, D.C., the Norfolk area, and towns all over the Eastern Shore and Delaware. Most of those convicted in the following days and weeks were ordered to pay fines of between $50 and $100.

As for Private First Class Baker, he was taken to Peninsula General Hospital in Salisbury and treated for a concussion. He, too, was convicted of disorderly conduct. His fine was set at $550, but the judge suspended $250 of that amount. After his family paid the fine, Baker was escorted back to Camp LeJeune by a Marine sergeant. (I tried to find on the internet news of what happened to him later in life, but alas, that search turned up empty.)

There was one last flare-up on that infamous Labor Day weekend, though this one ended on a humorous note. On Sunday, police had an encounter with another teen who was on the boardwalk but not wearing a shirt. Back in 1960, that qualified as a violation of city ordinances.

The police led that young man off of the boardwalk and onto the beach, where going shirtless was not a crime. While doing this, the officers found themselves surrounded by a crowd of 500 teens. Some angry shouts filled the air, but cooler heads prevailed. In impromptu fashion, the teens broke into a pair of sing-a-longs. First came "Hail, Hail the Gang's All Here." That was followed by "The Beer Barrel Polka." This follow-up "riot" lasted just 15 minutes.

In public statements about the Labor Day riots, town

officials tried to walk the line between criticizing the teenagers involved in the riot and not alienating young people in general, who then and now make up a big part of their tourism market.

City Council President Harry Kelly: *I suppose this was bound to happen sooner or later. We've kept the lid on teenagers pretty tight all summer. I guess the pressure had to give.*

Worcester County Commissioner (and former Ocean City mayor) Daniel Trimper said he thought that the police handled the situation in an "OK" manner but then added:

We want young people here. They are the future of Ocean City.

Early on, Mayor Cropper had harsh things to say about the rioters, but he, too, calmed down as the days went on.

We want to attract young people. We want to make the city and the boardwalk attractive to all age groups, but we simply cannot tolerate rowdyism.

The tourism season came to an end that weekend. There was no more trouble along these lines in Ocean City during the months that followed. Soon enough, the summer of 1961 would arrive.

THE JAILBREAK KING
OF DELMARVA

The criminal career of Gilbert Lare, aka "The Del-Mar-Va Bandit," began with a seemingly minor affair. Here is the *Wilmington News Journal*, Dec. 27, 1926:

> *Gilbert Lare, a young man of [Federalsburg, Md.], was arrested by Constable Thomas Nichols [and charged with] breaking into [Leon Todd's] store on South Main Street Wednesday night and removing two slot machines. ... The machines were found early the following morning along the river shores, broken up, and nearly $40 in quarters and nickels removed from them.*

There is not much in this incident that hints at the daring and brazen escapades that would soon follow. Still, I can't help but wonder if either Lare or Constable Nichols had a clue during the chase leading up to this arrest that their cops-and-robbers relationship would continue through most of the next decade. From the same article:

> *When the arrest was made Lare was some distance out of Federalsburg, walking toward Bridgeville, [Del.]. On being hailed by Constable Nichols, who caught up to him in a car,*

[Lare] at once took to flight and ran through Tanyard Branch, a stream of water crossing the road. After a short pursuit up the bed of the branch, he was overtaken and subdued.

The Earliest of the Houdini Escapes
Constable Nichols locked Lare up in the Federalsburg jail. Lare escaped. He was captured in Seaford, Del. and put in jail there. He escaped again. The following summer, the 20-year-old was back in jail after getting nabbed while trying to sell typewriters he had stolen from Wicomico High School. Lare had a thing for office supplies.

The *Salisbury Daily Times*, Aug. 19, 1927: *Gilbert Lare, who escaped from jails at Seaford, Del. and Federalsburg, Md., made an unsuccessful attempt to saw his way from the Wicomico County jail yesterday. Lare had sawed one of the iron bars in the south window at both ends and could have removed it with little effort in a few minutes. After darkness, he could [have crawled] out through the window and gained his freedom. A small saw about one-and-a-half inches in length and a knife with knicked blades used to sever the bar were found in the cell by the sheriff.*

Lare reached a deal with prosecutors, admitting to "receiving stolen goods" without pleading guilty to the burglary and larceny charges. I did not find any story about the final sentence, but soon enough, he was back at his chosen vocation. He was arrested in Wilmington on July 3, 1928 while trying to unload tools and supplies he had pilfered from a school in Delmar, Md. Delaware authorities turned Ware over to their colleagues in Maryland, but Ware promptly escaped from the jail in Delmar.

If you are keeping score, that is three jailbreaks in a year and a half for a young man barely out of his teens.

'An Apt Student of the Magical Influence of Houdini'

In December 1928, Lare found himself on the second floor of the jail in Salisbury, Md. after being arrested for stealing typewriters from Wicomico High School.

The *Salisbury Daily Times*, Dec. 12, 1928: *Hacksaws, blanket ropes, and sawed steel bars figured prominently in a spectacular ... jailbreak early this morning when Gilbert Lare, [21], and Dalton Smith, 17, escaped from the southwest cell of the Wicomico County prison. ... Lare, whose uncanny faculties for escaping from Eastern Shore jails has made him an apt student of the magical influence of the late Houdini, is believed to have engineered and executed the escape.*

The pair used a saw to cut through the bars on a window, creating an opening just wide enough for a man's shoulders. Their work was discovered only when city police officers passed outside the building and saw those "blanket ropes" hanging from a second-story window.

Dalton Smith was captured a few days later. He would be sentenced to a couple of years in reform school. But Lare proved a bigger challenge, even with his old nemesis Constable Nichols on the case.

The *Wilmington News Journal*, Dec. 17, 1928: *Constable Thomas L. Nichols [of Federalsburg], remembering Lare's penchant for coming to his former home after his escapes, watched for him [with the help of] two state troopers, but not until night did they get on the fugitive's trail. Hearing that he was in a colored barbershop ... north of [town], the officers hurried there, but as they entered the front door Lare slipped out the rear and sprinted into the woods, and since then has not been seen.*

(A point of clarification: Gilbert Lare seems to have made a habit of hiding and hanging out in black neighborhoods, but he was, in fact, a white man.)

The Del-Mar-Va Bandit Gets Downright Playful

Here is where the story of Gilbert Lare takes a turn worthy of a Hollywood movie about a charismatic antihero who takes joy in taunting the police officers on his trail.

The *Wilmington News Journal*, Jan. 4, 1929: *Roy Drew, a citizen of Federalsburg, received a souvenir postcard [from the Delmarva jail-breaker] Gilbert Lare a day or so ago, postmarked Daytona, Florida and on which Lare had written: "Tell Constable Thomas Nichols that if he had looked closer he would have caught me."*

Though never confirmed, police developed a theory that Lare had skedaddled in the company of another legendary Delmarva criminal, Alfred Brittingham, whose specialty was stealing cars.

The *Wilmington News Journal*, Jan. 5, 1929: *No cars have been reported stolen, no holdups perpetrated, and all tips as to Brittingham's whereabouts have proven baseless. [Brittingham] had been traveling through the peninsula, picking up a new car [whenever] the one he was driving ran out of gas. Abandoned and undamaged cars blazed his trail through Somerset, Wicomico, and Worcester counties.*

That postcard was not the only missive Lare sent while on the lam. He also mailed a playful Christmas card directly to his old nemesis, Constable Nichols. In it, he promised to return to town soon, adding:

"Watch out for me."

In this case, Gilbert Lare was a man of his word.

The *Wilmington Evening Journal*, Jan. 17, 1929: *The looting of the fertilizer warehouse office of Herman Wright [in Feder-*

alsburg] and the theft of a large truck is taken by local officers as mute evidence of the return of Gilbert Lare, the Peninsula's champion jailbreaker, to his home, just as he promised on a Christmas card to a local officer. The man who is credited with saying that he has broken out of every jail on the Peninsula has been as large since his break from the Salisbury jail several weeks ago.

Lare had stolen that truck and then driven it to Herman Wright's office, backing it up to a loading dock and packing up every bit of office furniture in the joint—chairs, adding machines, typewriters, and more.

From the same article: *An office stripped of all furnishings with the exception of a heavy safe and the swinging doors of a warehouse stood as testimonials today of the daring of a man of whom residents along the Eastern Shore speak respectfully for his many accomplishments.*

There are two humorous extras to this escapade. First, Lare had already committed this exact same crime. The goods stolen on one of his early heists had been discovered and returned. Now, he was stealing the same items again. Also, just before pulling off this repeat heist, Lare had engaged in conversation with some "colored men" gathered along the railroad tracks that ran through Federalsburg. He pointed to lights on in a distant office and told those men:

"I see Herman Wright and R.O. Dean have got their lights on—[they] must be scared somebody will break in and steal."
Then he added: *"The next time I leave Federalsburg I'll take half the town with me."*

Busted by a Vigilant Farmer
The next day, Jan. 18, the headline in the *Evening Journal* read: "Outlaw Caught in Kent, Co., Md."

His capture was affected by the suspicion of H.W. McMahon, [a Kent County farmer] ... who recognized the truck of G.T. Bell and Son [when it] stopped at McMahon's place, near Chestertown. After [Lare] drove away, McMahon called the sheriff of Kent County, Md., and officers were sent in pursuit."

The stolen goods were still inside when the police pulled that truck over. Gilbert Lare was soon back in jail, this time in Denton.

By a number of people [in Federalsburg] who have known the boy since his childhood it is thought that he cannot help committing the acts and that possibly an operation on the brain might correct his apparently unconquerable mania for breaking in and stealing.

The *Wilmington News Journal*, Jan. 22, 1929: *The sentiment is growing that Lare should be given a mental examination at some institution by experts to ascertain if pressure on the brain or some other ailment is the cause of his criminal tendencies. It is pointed out that after breaking into a place he makes no effort to cover up his tracks, and in a short time will appear in that town, on the streets.*

Even Houdini Can't Escape from the Denton Jail

By this point, you know that Gilbert Lare tried his very best to live up to his jailbreaker reputation, but he was unable to escape from the Caroline County Detention Center in Denton, Md.

The *Wilmington News Journal*, Jan. 22, 1929: *Lare was foiled Sunday night in an attempt to escape from the Denton jail. [He] had taken up the floor of his cell and was about to get away by a drainpipe when he was frustrated by the alertness of Sheriff Jackson. The youthful offender was then placed in a specially constructed steel cage [that is usually reserved for murderers.] It is believed [this cell] will hold him.*

Guess who came to visit Gilbert Lare in the Denton jail? His old friend and nemesis from the Federalsburg police force.

The *Wilmington News Journal*, Feb. 8, 1929: *[When] visited by Constable Thomas L. Nichols of Federalsburg yesterday, [Lare] said: "I wish they'd hurry up and try me and send me where I'm going. I am making no headway at all in this place!"*

In early March, rumors spread like wildfire that Gilbert Lare had escaped again. Caroline County Sheriff Jackson felt obliged to give interviews to reporters so as to assure the public that The Del-Mar-Va Bandit was still inside that cage reserved for murderers, though not for lack of trying on his part.

The *Wilmington News Journal*, March 6, 1929: *In the last few days the Del-Mar-Va bandit removed several long, flat pieces of iron on which run the wheels of the sliding doors of the special steel cage in which he is held, and hid them in his bed, but they were discovered.*

A Stay in the Maryland Penitentiary

The *Wilmington News Journal*, April 8, 1929: *Gilbert 'Dicky' Lare, 22-year-old Federalsburg youth ... who has achieved the title of the 'Del-Mar-Va Bandit' in the past four years, was sentenced to two years in the Maryland Penitentiary.*

After Lare served that sentence, things stayed quiet for several years. He returned to the Federalsburg area. He took on real jobs as a carpenter. But in the end, he wasn't ready to give up on a life of crime.

The *Wilmington News Journal*, Nov. 6, 1934: *Gilbert "Dickie" Lare of Federalsburg who three or four years ago made a reputation in a large area of the Peninsula as a result of his implication in robberies and jailbreaks ... is suspected of having been the brains of a series of recent robberies. Lare was arrested yesterday after William Edwards, a Norfolk Negro, is alleged to have confessed his part in the robbery of Covey & Williams hardware store.*

Later in the same article: *[Lare] engineered the robbery and gained entrance to the hardware store by placing a ladder against a high window. Edwards was captured after Constable Nichols and Officer Floyd Phillips chased him through cornfields. Two Negroes [also] alleged to have been involved are still at large.*

The next year brought more of the same.

The *Wilmington News Journal*, Oct. 7, 1935: *Gilbert Lare, a Federalsburg youth, is charged with having broken into and robbed the storehouse of Jacob O. Williams, hardware and automobile dealer.*

And the year after that, still more of the same.

The *Wilmington News Journal*, Dec. 1, 1936: *Committed to the local lock-up when arrested for questioning in the recent triple store robbery [in Federalsburg], Gilbert 'Dickie' Lare, sometimes called champion jailbreaker of the Eastern Shore... proved true to form in attempting to break his bonds, although his attempt was foiled by police. ... Removing some of the jail's plumbing pipes to use as tools, he managed to break and remove several cement blocks from the building as a means of exit when his work was detected just in time.*

As an old newspaperman myself, I have to give props here to the anonymous writer of this article who, in recounting Lare's long history of escapes, employs Gilbert Lare's nickname in describing him as "the slippery Dickie."

The Bandit's Trail Ends … Or Does it?

Presumably, Lare was sent back to the penitentiary for a while, though I have not come across confirmation of that in old newspapers. The trail of the Del-Mar-Va bandit runs pretty cold after this, though there is a possibility that Lare eventually settled in Salisbury, began working again as a carpenter, and lived a mostly crime-free life. Fifteen years after that last arrest above, this intriguing item popped up in the *Salisbury Daily Times* of April 5, 1951:

> *[A Salisbury man was] jailed by City Police yesterday on breach of trust charges. Gilbert Lare, 46, of Camden Ave. and Market St., is being held in lieu of $1,000 bond. He is charged by Harold L. Porter, … an appliance dealer, with a breach of trust totaling $65.*

The age is about right, but I do not know if this was the same Gilbert Lare. Nor do I know for sure if an obituary that appeared in the *Salisbury Daily Times* on Nov. 24, 1976 is for the same Gilbert Lare. The obituary describes a 72-year-old man, which is in the ballpark of the age "The Del-Mar-Va Bandit" would have been. The brief article describes him as a "retired cabinetmaker," which fits with his earlier forays into carpentry work. But it puts his birthplace at Hurlock, Md. and makes no mention of Federalsburg.

Nor, of course, does it make mention of the spectacular, headline-grabbing exploits of "The Del-Mar-Va Bandit." This Gilbert Lare–again, it may or may not be the same man–had two daughters and three grandchildren. If he was the Bandit, here's hoping he grew up into an outstanding (and upstanding) family patriarch.

THE SHIP THAT BROUGHT SHAME TO POCOMOKE

The Pocomoke City, Md. shipyard of E. James Tull was quite the famous operation, both in his day and in the annals of Delmarva history. After rising through the ranks at shipyards in his native Somerset County, Tull launched his own shipbuilding operation in 1884. His yard spanned an era of great change in the industry. He built vessels ranging from bugeyes to gas-powered yachts.

Chesapeake Bay Maritime Museum curator and historian Pete Lesher wrote a great piece about the shipyard for a museum publication back in 2007. Here is one bit of Lesher's bottom line:

Overall, Tull built a remarkable variety of vessels—bugeyes, schooners, sloops, skipjacks, fish steamers, tugs, motor freight boats, schooner barges, launches, sailing and power yachts, barges, and a ram—some 200 in all, by a claim in his own 1917 advertisement. Measured either by number of hulls or total tonnage launched, no Eastern Shore shipbuilder out produced him.

By all accounts, Tull loved his adopted hometown. He served as mayor for a long time. He contributed to countless civic causes. And yes his shipyard produced a vessel that put that town's name in unflattering headlines all across the country.

The *Pocomoke* Gets Busted

In 1921, the Tull-built schooner *Pocomoke* was seized off the coast of New Jersey in a "spectacular raid." Its crew was charged with bringing a huge shipment of liquor to the East Coast during prohibition times. Search archives of old newspapers for articles about the case, and you will find hundreds of hits from papers near and far.

Federal agents didn't actually find any booze on board. They knew that the *Pocomoke* had loaded up more than $50,000 worth of the stuff while in the Caribbean. That booze was supposedly headed for Canada. But before the boat showed up in Canada, it appeared off the coast of New Jersey. There was no liquor aboard.

The crew had an oh-so-harrowing tale to tell about this. There was such a big storm! We were all going to drown! The only way to stay afloat was to dump all that liquor overboard!

No one believed them. Everyone knew they had unloaded the liquor onto smaller, rum-running speedboats while anchored outside the famous "three-mile limit" where prohibition laws didn't apply.

Within a few months, the crew would all give up on their stormy lies and plead guilty.

The *Worcester Democrat and Ledger Enterprise* of Pocomoke City wrote up one of its stories on the incident this way:

The schooner Pocomoke, *which was recently built by Mr. E. James Tull of this city at his shipyard here, has brought herself into prominence and at the same time put Pocomoke City on the map ... Many of our people remember the launching of the* Pocomoke *in this city sometime since, but at the time little did they think that she would come into such prominence. Judging from the dryness of our town it is safe to say that none of her cargo ever found its way to the port of her birth.*

The embarrassing headlines for Pocomoke City kept on coming in the years that followed. In December 1924, the *Pocomoke* was pulled over by the destroyer *Jouett* off the coast of Connecticut. Those investigators found 1,200 cases of liquor in the cargo hold. Four months after that, the *Pocomoke* reappeared off the coast of Connecticut—this time she was carrying more than 1,000 cases of liquor.

One Very Big Footnote

I came across a very strange side story to that 1921 incident while looking into this. I am just going to reprint it here—it was on the front page of the *Philadelphia Inquirer* on Oct 7, 1921.

Rum Schooner Sailor Makes Plea for Shoes

Special Order Necessary to Cover Pedal Extremities of Prisoner

Kenneth Roberts, the big sailor from the schooner Pocomoke *which is now in the custody of the government because it carried a rum cargo, has now decided that he needs shoes. He has not worn shoes since he was taken off of the* Pocomoke *three months ago and claims that he has not worn them for years, but he finds that the weather is getting too cold and that the cold floor in the detention house of the Bureau of Immigration, where he was taken on Monday from Trenton, is not very inviting to bare feet.*

He made application today for shoes to Commissioner Hughes. His feet are so big that no shoes are to be had in stock, so a local shoemaker will be asked to make him a pair.

Firebug! Madness in Early Cape Charles

The town of Cape Charles, Va. took shape in the mid-1880s as a meticulously planned community built around a newly construct-ed railroad line. Lots of smart people had doubts about the plan, as its success depended on a proposition that seemed quite iffy in those years. The railroad line claimed it would keep costs within reason by loading dozens of railway cars directly onto barges and towing them behind tug boats across the Chesapeake Bay to Norfolk.

Barges were being used to move railway cars in other places by then, but mostly for short distances within the confines of protected harbors. The Cape Charles plan involved towing those cars across 36 miles of open water. They made it work, thanks in no small part to the engineering skills of project planner Alexander Cassatt. Trains started running through Cape Charles in late 1884. The town was officially incorporated in the spring of 1886.

There were moments of Wild-West mayhem in those heady early days. In August 1887, a melee broke out among hard-drinking fishermen that involved "double-barrel shotguns, repeating rifles, and pistols." At least five were wounded," and "the women and children were very much alarmed." Mayor Allen Smith resigned in the wake of that shootout—and several others to boot.

Debt, Confusion, Madness: A Civic Leader Loses His Way
But the moment of craziness that I want to focus on here is a sadder affair that speaks to the fragile nature of the human mind. One of the town's early entrepreneurs, J.J. Bunting, liked to play the real estate market. Within a short time after his arrival in 1886, he had scooped up several downtown buildings, including the Cape Charles Hotel.

The fact that Bunting's name is mostly forgotten now is mostly a matter of luck. In January of 1889, he hired a man to set fire to one of his downtown buildings.

• If the guy he'd hired had been more competent ...

• Or if the fire hadn't been discovered so quickly by alert neighbors ...

• Or if the guests at the nearby Arlington Hotel hadn't so generously jumped in to help ...

• Or if the wind had picked up just so ...

In any of those cases, an out-of-control blaze might well have consumed Cape Charles in its infancy, just as so many other blazes devastated so many other Delmarva towns in those days of wooden construction and bucket brigades.

This fire didn't do any serious damage. But the news that Bunting was involved in starting the blaze stunned Cape Charles. Bunting was a civic bigwig. He had served on the city council. He was a member of the Masons and the Knights of Pythias. He owned all those buildings.

To make matters worse, his motive made no sense whatsoever. From the *Richmond Dispatch* on Jan. 23, 1889:

Your correspondent ...visited Cape Charles today to attend the preliminary trial of J. J. Bunting, arrested upon the charge, according to his own confession, of having caused the fire in the central portion of the place on Thursday morning of last week, which but for its timely discovery would have resulted in the destruction of the entire business part of the town. The facts as developed were both surprising and mysterious, and led to the belief that Bunting must have been temporarily insane—his insanity caused by his carrying considerable debt.

Bunting hired a man named Samuel Roane to burn the Masonic lodge. Bunting had an insurance policy worth $4,000 on that building. Somehow, he had worked himself into a frenzy over the possibility that the insurance company was going to cancel his policy. *The Dispatch* again:

The Commonwealth's Attorney says it is one of the most mysterious crimes that has come under his notice [over] the past 18 years, because, from a financial standpoint, there was no excuse for burning the property. It could have been sold at any time for $5,000.

In addition to that, Bunting owned some $4,000 of other property in the same block that would have been burned had the fire gotten under full headway, and [those latter properties] had but a small amount of insurance.

How did Bunting's thoughts get so out of whack? Did he suffer all along from a well-hidden mental illness? Did he have some sort of breakdown? Or did his mind just get all tangled up in a web of nonsense? The townsfolk didn't have any answers to those questions. Here is *The Dispatch*, again:

His downfall is a surprise to everyone, and created great

sympathy for his wife and children, who are almost heartbroken at the turn in affairs. It was one of the saddest scenes ever witnessed when he was taken from his home tonight to be carried to the jail, and stout-hearted men shed tears for the sorrowing and grief-stricken family.

Bunting did time in the state penitentiary. So far, I have been unable to find out what happened to him later in life.

We know what happened to the town he tried to burn, however. Bunting's interlude of madness was just a blip of tragic news in an extraordinary civic success story. From a marshy, uninhabited wasteland in 1883, Cape Charles grew to 300 residents in 1885, 800 in 1887, and more than 1,000 in 1900.

FLIRTATION TO FURY: THE CHOCOLATE CANDY MURDERS

If Shakespeare had written tragedies in early 1900s America instead of early 1600s Britain, he would have had another character named Cordelia to write about. The plot he might have put together from the story of Cordelia Botkin would begin in a flash of flirtatious excitement that soon blossoms into passionate-but-illicit romance. Alas, the closing acts of that drama would sink relentlessly into betrayal, jealousy, fury, madness, and murder.

When Cordelia Botkin died in 1910, the official autopsy report attributed her demise to "softening of the brain due to melancholy." She was serving a life sentence in prison at the time.

From Flirtation to Philandering

The story of this Cordelia's downfall begins not on the Delmarva Peninsula, but on the West Coast. San Francisco was in its pre-earthquake glory days on the early 1890s day that found Cordelia relaxing on a bench in popular Golden Gate Park. A handsome young man pedaled toward her on a bicycle. Did she feel a shiver of sexual temptation when that bike broke down and the rider dismounted to do repairs?

She gestured, inviting him to come over and talk. Social norms were different then—launching a casual chat with a passing stranger was not "acceptable" behavior for an unattached woman. Who can say for sure what went through that bike rider's mind? Perhaps he suspected, even hoped, where this reckless invitation might lead. That day marked the start of a romance that stretched through one year, then two, and into a third.

John Presley Dunning is not the hero of this drama. For starters, he was married. He was a bit of a con man as well. The native of Middletown, Del. worked as an itinerant journalist. Among his early jobs was a stint with the *Wilmington News Journal*. That's where he met his bride, Elizabeth Pennington. She hailed from a prominent family. Her father, John B. Pennington, had served as attorney general and U.S. congressman. The Pennington's impressive home in Dover stood right up against the "Dover Green," then and now the heart of the state capitol complex.

Back to John Dunning. In addition to his local newspaper work, Dunning did time as a foreign correspondent. In 1889, he scored a gigantic scoop as the first journalist to confirm that a typhoon had ripped through the Pacific island of Samoa, destroying several U.S. and German warships and killing more than 200 sailors.

Only one telegraph office was running on the island in the wake of the storm. To prevent other reporters from getting their news of the tragedy out, Dunning paid premium emergency rates to clog up that telegraph line with an endless run of Bible verses. I came across one report that said he paid an astonishing $8,000 in fees on that stunt, but it paid off. His name became known in national journalism circles. He soon got an offer to become the head honcho at the San Francisco office of the Associated Press newswire.

This is how the newlywed Dunnings came to settle in the City by the Bay. Elizabeth gave birth to a daughter, Mary, before the couple celebrated their first anniversary.

If John Dunning had turned out to be a top-notch journalist, that telegraph stunt he pulled might seem in retrospect like an entertaining display of competitive ingenuity. But Dunning was not destined for greatness. He had a big-time gambling problem. He might have been a thief, too, as he lost that big AP job amid whispers about embezzling.

It gets worse: Dunning was a serial philanderer. More on that later, except to say that his wife grew sick and tired of the mess Dunning made of everything in San Francisco. Divorce was not really a viable option in those days. Elizabeth and little Mary moved back to Dover, settling in at her father's house.

It was in this window that Dunning hopped on his bicycle and pedaled through Golden Gate Park. Like most philanderers through history, Dunning played the sob-story card. He told Cordelia that his wife didn't understand him. She was too religious, he complained, and she kept trying to force him to abide by moral standards that were "too high for me."

Cordelia responded with lies. She told Dunning she was a 29-year-old widow. She was 41, actually, and separated from her still-breathing husband.

With Elizabeth 3,000 miles away in Delaware, Dunning moved into Cordelia's place. He didn't have any money to speak of, but the lovers lost a lot of her money on horse races. They spent evenings in brazen extramarital socializing, barhopping, and theater-going to their heart's content.

Someone in San Francisco played the role of tattletale.

Several anonymous letters arrived at the Pennington house in Dover, informing Elizabeth about her husband's betrayal with an unnamed woman. Elizabeth's father intercepted most of those missives, trying to shield his daughter from further anguish. That John B. Pennington held onto those letters instead of throwing them away would become an important bit of evidence in sorting out the tragic events that soon unfolded.

That Deadly Box of Candy

The romance between Cordelia Botkin and John Presley Dunning hit the rocks after the Spanish American War broke out in the spring of 1898. The Associated Press needed all hands on deck, especially hands with foreign-correspondent experience. Dunning headed where the action was, hoping that the war would help get his career back on track. At first he wrote regularly to Cordelia. But then the missives became fewer and further between. His tone grew colder. Eventually, Dunning broke the news to his lover that he planned to return to Dover and give his marriage to Elizabeth another try.

That brings us to Aug. 9, 1898. The menu for dinner that night at the Pennington house in Dover included fried trout and corn fritters. Afterward, Elizabeth's 14-year-old nephew Harry Pennington went to get the mail. He returned with a wrapped box labeled "Bonbons." They were a gift for Elizabeth. The postmark was San Francisco. Inside was a note: "With love to yourself and the baby." It was signed "Mrs. C." Elizabeth assumed they were from "Mrs. Corbaly," a friend from her San Francisco days.

Elizabeth dug into those chocolates. So did several other family members and visiting friends. Everyone who ate chocolate got sick. There was lots of vomiting. The patients complained bitterly of heat, but their skin was cold to the touch. Two days later,

Elizabeth's sister, Leila Deane, died. Elizabeth died on the third day. Everyone else recovered.

The family's doctor said a batch of corn fritters gone bad was to blame. But as a lawyer who had prosecuted his share of crimes, John B. Pennington didn't buy that theory. He sent samples of the chocolates to his friend Theodore R. Worf, the state chemist and a professor at Delaware College (which would eventually become the University of Delaware). Worf found arsenic grains in the mix. Autopsies later showed that both women had ingested enough arsenic "to have killed a horse."

One of the investigators assigned to the case, Bernard J. McVey, went looking for clues from experienced shippers in the chocolate game. A Wilmington candy shop suggested he get in touch with another business in Philadelphia that manufactured candy boxes. The shipping department in that business pointed the finger at Haas & Sons Confectionary in San Francisco. Clerks at that store recalled a little bit about a woman who'd bought those chocolates and shipped them to Delaware.

Meanwhile, the bereaved-if-unfaithful husband of Elizabeth Dunning had departed the war zone and returned to San Francisco. There, he told police that the handwriting on the note that arrived with the chocolates matched that of his paramour, Cordelia Botkin.

The Media Goes Bananas
Do you hate getting a jury summons, or a call to testify in court? Well, imagine how the Delawareans involved in this case felt when the governor of California refused to extradite Cordelia Botkin to Delaware and insisted the trial unfold in San Francisco. To give testimony, they were legally obliged to ride trains across the county and spend weeks living out of a hotel. California spent

$3,000 on transportation, lodging, and living expenses for six Delaware witnesses. The hotels involved did not yet have high-speed internet connections.

The trial lasted a month. The jury deliberated for two hours. They found Botkin guilty.

What a month it was in the media! The San Francisco Examiner was owned during the 1890s by William Randolph Hearst, a name linked in the annals of newspapering with the brand of over-the-top sensationalism known as "yellow journalism." Hearst's papers chased controversy, not news. They hired reporters whose mission was selling newspapers, not getting facts straight.

Hearst got filthy rich with that approach. He was the model for *Citizen Kane* in the famous Orson Welles film. Newspapers all over the country soon followed Hearst's lead, filling their pages with screaming headlines and shameless innuendo.

Sex, infidelity, murder, jealousy—the Botkin story was tailor-made for the yellow journalism era. When the *San Francisco Chronicle* published an array of sketches and photographs of Botkin, they did so with this snide comment:

They indicate plainly the woman's excessive vanity and her fondness for posing.

When word broke about the chocolates coming from that Haas confectionary, so many journalists descended on the place that staff members went into hiding. A similar mad rush followed the news that a handkerchief in the chocolate box had been traced to the City of Paris department store.

The public couldn't get enough stories about the case. Overflow crowds arrived outside the courthouse every morning, hoping to land a seat in the courtroom. On one rainy day, clouds of steam formed in the courtroom from the dampness of soaked clothing. The interest seemed especially intense on the distaff side of the gender aisle:

Never before has there been such a fluttering of petticoats in court.

On the day of closing arguments, more than 500 people were turned away from the jam-packed courtroom. The *Examiner* set up a giant bulletin board on the streets outside the courtroom where they posted snippet summaries of what was going on inside.

John Presley Dunning had a bad time of it on the witness stand. He tried oh-so-hard to play the role of grieving husband, but it's hard to pull that off while fielding questions about your history of infidelity. The ladies in attendance who might have expected magnetism and sex appeal in Cordelia's philandering lover were disappointed by his whiny voice and thinning hair.

Asked by defense lawyers if he had been intimate with women other than Botkin during his time in San Francisco, Dunning said yes. Asked how many, he said, "Many." Pressed, he said there were too many to remember. Pressed further, he confessed to extramarital escapades with at least six women. Asked to name them, he said he couldn't remember. Pushed, he said he could recall three names, but insisted that he was too much of a gentleman to reveal names.

Dunning spent a couple of nights in jail for refusing to give those names, but the defense attorneys eventually agreed to just drop the question.

Cordelia took the stand, too. In one journalists' judgment, she was "long on looks and feminine charm, short on gray matter." She offered up a series of alibis when it came to buying arsenic and sending the chocolate, but the jury didn't buy them for a second. She told the court that she had taken morphine on the day the chocolates were mailed and stayed alone in her room all day, as she was "thoroughly unfit" to be seen in public.

Lots of legal maneuvering unfolded in the wake of the quick guilty verdict, but none of it mattered. A court overturned the verdict over questions about jury tampering, but Botkin was convicted again after a second trial. Her lawyers tried to get her a third trial, but they failed. Cordelia Botkin was sentenced to life in jail.

The Return of the Temptress

While testifying in court, Cordelia Botkin tried to present herself as shy and polite. Once in jail, she seems to have jumped right back into her preferred role of seductress. One day in April 1900 Judge Carroll Cook was riding one of San Francisco's streetcars along Guerrero Street when he was stunned to see a familiar face. Convicted murderess Cordelia Botkin was dressed to the nines and riding that car in the company of a man who appeared to be her date.

The judge launched a formal inquiry. The Delaware newspapers went ballistic with outraged headlines. Here is what eventually got revealed:

• Botkin received an array of special privileges from her jail guards. She was allowed to dress in her glamorous clothes. She was given the freedom to stroll outside the prison building and visit the facility's gardens whenever she liked. She ate her meals privately, away from the general prison population.

• She went on multiple field trips into San Francisco. The county sheriff claimed that these field trips were supervised affairs with a guard always nearby, but Judge Cook had not seen a guard on the streetcar, and no one seems to have believed that sheriff for a second.

You Wouldn't Believe!

• The guy Judge Cook had seen Botkin with on the street-car was indeed a date. Smitten with the murderess, this man had attended every day of her trial. He then got in touch with her in jail, and the lovebirds soon arranged a rendezvous despite her life sentence.

• Two prison guards had gotten into a furious fistfight over Botkin. One guard had threatened to expose the fact that the other was having an affair with Botkin. The smitten guard, Frank McFarland, beat that other man nearly to death. Media reports claimed that McFarland walked away from that fight calm as could be, whistling a ragtime tune.

One newspaper dubbed Botkin "the siren of the branch county jail."

The walls started to close in on Botkin as all this came to light. Her special privileges were revoked. Her lawyers said there were no more appeals to file. The parole board offered no hope. Her only son passed away, suddenly. Botkin sank into depression. The warden at her prison said:

For some time she had said that she wanted to die.

Two nurses were assigned to make sure that the prisoner ate some food and took her medicines every day. She passed away in March of 1910. That was two years after the death of her one-time paramour, William Dunning. He was 44 years old and living in Philadelphia at the time of his passing. I have not been able to find much of anything about Dunning's life and activities in the years after the murders.

When reporting on the death of Cordelia Botkin, the *Evening Times* newspaper of Alameda, Calif. was not in a kindly mood:

Whatever beauty [she] may have possessed ... had long since departed.

Postscripts: Murder by Mail Oddities

If you are visiting Dover and want to pay your respects to the victims here, Elizabeth Pennington Dunning and her sister are buried in the old Presbyterian cemetery in Dover. That graveyard is near the Dover Green, at 316 Governors Avenue. The home where the Penningtons lived is now known as the "Paton House." The Delaware State Housing Authority has offices there. I believe that some of the walking tours put together by the First State Heritage Park feature this site in the itinerary.

• This next postscript is too strange not to share. Though born in Missouri, Cordelia Botkin had spent nearly all of her life in California. As we've seen, the sensational story of her crimes landed her on the front pages of newspapers around the country. Upon her death in 1910, the *Daily Press* of Sheboygan, Wisc. included this tidbit, which I share despite (or, perhaps, because of) its hard-to-believe quality:

Mrs. Botkin's father and mother did not know that she had died in prison. They did not know that she had ever seen the inside of a prison anywhere, and they never heard of the Botkin case, which was one of the most famous criminal cases ever tried on the Pacific Coast. There is a little paper in the village where Mrs. Botkin's old father and mother lived, and the paper printed every day accounts of the trial when it was going on. But they called it the Dunning case and [referred to] Mrs. Botkin [always] as "the accused," and the old man and the old woman read the paper and talked the famous murder case over together and never even dreamed that "the accused" was their own daughter. And all the little village took hold of hands and formed around the old people a cordon of silence, and woe to anyone who dared to try to break through. We are prone to think of heaven as a place far removed from everything we know here on this earth. But, oh that little village out there, nestling in the green, green hills of smiling California! I wonder if the angels do not look down upon it and smile.

Botkin is buried at Oak Mound Cemetery in Healdsburg, Calif.

• The Delaware newspaperman Joe Martin had an interesting observation about the Botkin case. In the 1950s, he had a regular column called *Ramblin' Round with Joe Martin* in the *Wilmington Morning News*. He wondered aloud in one column about whether Cordelia Botkin had invented an entirely new method of killing—murder by mail.

That turns out to be not quite true. In 1891, a Rhode Island physician named Thomas Thatcher Graves sent some arsenic-laced whiskey to a rich heiress who had made Graves a beneficiary in her will. Botkin was the second-ever murderer by mail, so she missed that spot in the record book. But still: Her case is right near the starting point of a grisly little timeline that runs up to the Unabomber killings and anthrax mailings of more recent vintage.

You Wouldn't Believe!

STORMY WEATHER!

THE STARVING TIME ON HOLLAND ISLAND. OR NOT?

The new year of 1912 arrived on Delmarva with a frozen vengeance. In some places the ice stretched nearly unbroken from one shore of the Chesapeake Bay to the other. Rivers were impassable. Steamboats and sailboats were idled.

The deep freeze stretched through one whole week, then another, and then a third. Towns on the Eastern Shore endured troubles that went beyond bone-chilling temperatures. Groceries and other staples ran short on store shelves, though railroad lines remained open and served as a supply lifeline.

But those railroads couldn't help the families who lived in islands out in the middle of the Chesapeake Bay. Most such places didn't have telephone or telegraph lines yet. With no boats sailing, no one on the mainland knew how folks out on those islands were faring.

The focus of those worries soon became Holland Island, which is drowned today but then rose out of waters west of Deal Island, Md. Starting at Christmas, no one heard a peep of news from its 250ish residents. Then, in late January, Deal Islanders heard a thunderous run of noise from the direction of Holland. The gunshots rang out in long, clattering bursts. Then, silence. Then, more thunder. And so it went, almost all through the night.

The *Washington Times*, Feb. 5, 1912: *Persons here [on Deal Island] believe that the firing heard last night above the roar of grinding ice was the attempt of the people on the island to let the outside world know through the only means of communication they possess, that starvation, possibly death, faces their little community.*

From Fear to Panic

Deal is an island, too, but a short bridge crossing kept it connected with the mainland during this cold spell. Residents there started thinking back to the deep freezes of previous years and decades. Had an island in the Chesapeake ever been frozen out of contact with the outside world for this long? They didn't think so. Alarmed by that night of gunfire, they started sounding the alarm and demanding action from public officials.

That alarm soon reached the newsrooms of big-city papers in Baltimore and Washington, D.C., setting off a run of page-one headlines that stoked fears of an imminent humanitarian catastrophe. A few samples:

• *DANGER GROWS: Two Hundred And Fifty Inhabitants May Starve*

• *NO FOOD NOR PHYSICIAN: Marooned Nearly Five Weeks with No Word to the Outside*

• *HOLLAND ISLAND STILL IN NEED: No Doctors With Them and It Is Feared They May Have Died of Hunger and Sickness*

• *RESCUE SHIP ... SPEEDING TO ... RELIEF OF STARVING MEN*

You Wouldn't Believe!

Several Holland Islanders had gotten caught up on the mainland during Christmastime travels, unable to return home. Among them were the island's only doctor and its only preacher. The newspapers turned that news into word pictures filled with terrifying possibilities.

The *Baltimore Sun*, Feb. 5: *Fifty families comprising 250 men, women, and children ... for four weeks have been marooned from the mainland of Dorchester and Somerset counties, deprived of medical aid, cut off from food supplies, and are believed to be in circumstances bordering on starvation and death from disease, according to reports.*

A Halting Start to the Rescue

Then things got more frightening. A wicked storm rolled through. Nine oyster boats on Tilghman Island were swept out of protected Dogwood Harbor and into the Chesapeake Bay. That the captains and crew members aboard those vessels survived without a single fatality seemed like a miracle.

The *Baltimore Sun*, Feb. 5: *From all points along the Eastern Shore come stories of hardship and suffering. ... Paramount in the interest of Eastern Shoremen, however, is the welfare of the marooned Hollands Islanders. The fact that no word whatever has been received from the 250 souls on this island ... is causing much apprehension.*

Governor Emerson Harrington—an Eastern Shoreman himself, from Cambridge—jumped into the fray. But the first rescue vessel he sent, *Governor Thomas*, couldn't get through the ice and into the mouth of the Choptank River. The second boat was a bigger, rugged ice breaker called *Annapolis*. Alas, her struggle through the ice led into a stretch of Hoopers Straits where the water was too shallow for her draft. Next up was a 185-foot-long

U.S. Navy "cutter," *Apache*. The governor had to summon her captain, G.S. Carmine, back from leave in New York City.

While all this was going on, various would-be heroes stepped up to offer their services. Five duck hunters from Cecil County, Md. proclaimed themselves ready to make the trip in flat-bottomed boats fitted with ice-runners and sails. The celebrated young aviator Paul Peck announced that he would fly to the island if the new "airship" he had just built passed an upcoming flight test in College Park, Md. (Peck would die in an unrelated plane crash later this same year, at age 23.)

These offers were put on hold for *Apache*, which set off from Baltimore on Feb. 6 with two supply-laden steamships sailing in her ice-free wake. Newspaper reporters lodged aboard *Apache* filed blow-by-blow reports during the vessel's long, arduous sail down the Bay to Holland Island—the journey took 24 full hours.

Bracing for the Worst Possible News
Every day since hearing that thunderous run of gunfire, Deal Islanders had bundled up and headed out to the waterfront armed with telescopes, hoping to catch a glimpse of human activity on Holland Island.

Deal Island Deputy Sheriff W.J. Tankersley: *Those people, I know from conditions before the freeze-up, are now in dire want, and to be absolutely frank we can't tell whether they are dead or alive. ... Not a sign of a man or woman has been seen. I am positive that four weeks of privation has caused a small disaster, if not a calamity, on the island.*

The sheriff's opinion was widely shared, according to the *Baltimore Sun* of Feb. 5, 1912:

Residents of Deal Island, Oriole, Chance's Quarter, and

*the lower end of Dorchester county believe that unless immedi-
ate aid is given to the islanders it is most likely that many of them
will perish.*

As Marylanders breathlessly awaited news, the *Baltimore
Sun* pumped public anxiety with a long essay about the hardships
of life on Holland Island, both in general and in the current emergency. A few excerpts:

• *Many [people] there have never seen a trolley car or
moving picture.*

• *Every storm brings danger, every high wind the threat
of the elements to wipe out the settlement... To be on the island
during a strong northwesterly gale ... would cause a stranger to
shudder with fear.*

• *In the summer mosquitoes almost drive the inhabitants
insane. ... The mosquitoes are said to be the most poisonous in
existence.*

• *Picture it out—a place where freshwater is as precious
as any possession; where life is all but unbearable at best, with
fever-bearing mosquitoes in summer, isolation and starvation in
winter; with disease ever near, waiting for just such a chance;
food [supplies] never above immediate needs. Now—cut off from
food, medicine, fuel—for a whole month.*

• *It is thought that the people are now spending most of
their time in praying for assistance in their little chapel.*

The *Apache* Breaks Through at Last

Captain Carmine and his *Apache* pulled within sight of Holland Island at 8 in the morning on Wednesday, Feb. 7. Carmine
ordered a dozen men to row in on a smaller boat. The leader of
that rescue team, Lt. Boedecker, had this exchange with the first
islander he saw:

"Well, how's everything?"

"Oh, we're all right."

Boedecker then spied a gaggle of islanders. They were … ice skating, quite happily.

The *Baltimore Sun*, Feb. 8: *[The islanders] invited the officers of the cutter to join in the sport and remain with them for dinner. The revenue officers were somewhat chagrined [by the offer].*

When Boedecker offered to sail any islanders in need of safety to the mainland, he got no takers. When Capt. Carmine joined the scene, he mentioned that the *Apache* was loaded with emergency supplies.

[The islanders] expressed deep gratitude for the interest shown them by the visit, and asked that they be supplied with some lubricating oil and baking powder.

The *Baltimore Sun* reported on the investigation conducted by the crew of the Apache:

[It showed that] there were but one or two cases of illness, and these of not a serious nature; that there were sufficient provisions to last another four weeks; that the residents of the island had been having a good time, and that the greatest misfortune of the people had been that because of the absence of the minister, there had been no formal religious service … for more than a month.

Eventually, one of the rescuers asked about that thunderous gunfire, which had so alarmed the folks on Deal Island. That, the islanders explained, happened on a night when ducks and other waterfowl descended on Holland Island in huge numbers.

Last word from the *Baltimore Sun*: *It might have lent dramatic interest to the month of uncertainty since communication stopped if the islanders had been found starving and dying of pestilence, but that they were found enjoying good health and comparative plenty, notwithstanding the embargo of nature, has been made a matter of rejoicing.*

Postscript #1: *Apache* Gets Stuck

Upon hearing the shockingly good news from Holland Island, the Navy ordered *Apache* to proceed to Norfolk to join in the ceremonial launching of two new Navy cutters. Alas, the trip did not go well.

The *Washington Times*, Feb. 9: *After a night of ceaseless vigil on the part of Captain Carmine to prevent the United States revenue cutter* Apache *[from] being carried ashore by the heavy ice tides, the gallant little vessel finally gave up the fight at 7 o'clock this morning and became firmly wedged in the ice at Somers Cove in the Little Annemessex River. ... The* Times *reporter and photographer ... on the boat, were forced to clamber over her side onto 12 inches of solid ice and to make their way to shore.*

Postscript #2: A Voice of Reason

Lt. A.H. Scally of the *Apache* deserves some credit here for being a voice of reason. In all the articles I reviewed, he served up the lone quote that tried to tamp down the growing panic about starvation on Holland Island:

There are some adventurous characters among the oystermen, and I believe some of them [would] have put off for the mainland [by now] if they were suffering to any great extent.

Postscript #3: An Ode to the Survivors'

In those days, the *Baltimore Sun* had a "staff poet" named Folger McKinzey. A native of Cecil County on the Eastern Shore, he often wrote ditties celebrating the natural beauty and cultural charms of Delmarva. He whipped up this poem for publication the day after the news broke that the islanders weren't starving after all.

The Rescue of Holland Island

From Honga Strait to Tangier Sound
The cry of fear went up afar;
Deal's Island sent the wide alarm
By letter carrier, clerk, and tar:
"Those Holland Islanders are lost,
They're starved and dying day by day:
They're sick and frozen in their huts,
Oh, succor, succor, sirs, we pray!"

The heart of Maryland heard, and sprung
With ready will to give relief:
The Governor sent words of cheer,
The whole land joined the common grief.
The gallant Thomas did her best,
The iceboats sought the lower bay;
The lithe Apache through the field
of Arctic-bleakness broke her way.

At last, at last, an isle in sight!
"A mile southeast, and we'll be there
To lift them from their frozen night,
To save them from their dark despair!"
They heaved the lead, the line showed shoal,
But inch by inch they worked along;

You Wouldn't Believe!

The engines backed and went ahead,
The pistons answered every gong.

A half a mile, a quarter—joy!
The small boat lowered reaches land;
And there a hardy islander
Extends his brown and brawny hand.
The captain looks at him, looks he,
And eager to hear tales of woe,
Asks how the perishing have fared
In all that waste of ice and snow!

The native grins between dark teeth,
The native's eyes are twinkling bright:
"Come in! We're glad to see you, Cap!
Tie up your ship and spend the night!
We've got the nicest canvasback,
And fresh wild goose and terrapin!"
The captain threw up both his hands,
The crew swore black and blue as sin!

They stowed the bread and meat away,
They hid the medicine full deep;
They bade the islander good day,
And sought at last a wink of sleep.
Far o'er the waters rang the song
Of Holland's children, strait to strait:
"Why don't you stay to dinner, friend!
The finest ducks you ever ate!"

THE GREAT DELMARVA DEEP FREEZE OF 1977

Deep freezes used to be commonplace affairs on the Delmarva Peninsula. Newspapers and diaries from the 1700s, 1800s, and 1900s are stippled with reports of cold spells so deep that miles-wide rivers froze up nearly from shore to shore, to the point where schooners and even steamboats couldn't get through. When thaws began, giant ice floes rode the waves, toppling screwpile lighthouses and ripping oyster boats out of secure moorings.

As of this writing, nearly half a century has passed since the last genuine Delmarva deep freeze. But that last one was a doozy! Between mid-December 1976 and mid-February of 1977, the peninsula endured two months of temperatures so bone-chillingly cold that the National Oceanic and Atmospheric Agency rated it as the "coldest winter on the East Coast since maybe the founding of the Republic."

By Christmas Day the ice had started inching out from creeks and rivers into the Chesapeake Bay. The freeze soon reached into vast expanses of water that almost never see ice. The late photographer Bob Grieser took a famous shot showing dozens of people ice skating off the shores of Kent Island under the shadow of the Chesapeake Bay Bridge. Another of his shots has one kid driving a tractor on the ice, while the other hangs on for dear life atop the sled tied to that tractor.

Sharing the Misery: Snow in Miami!

Delmarva residents did not shiver alone that winter. During this same period, 49 East Coast cities recorded record low temperatures. Snow fell in the Miami area for the only time in recorded history. Incredibly, the same thing happened on Grand Bahama Island.

Meteorologists at the time were a bit mystified. Some attributed the freeze to a strange and out-of-place stretch of high pressure over the Mississippi River Valley, which forced to the south a cold front that in any normal season would have stayed hundreds of miles to the north.

Back on Delmarva, shipping in the Chesapeake and Delaware bays slowed to a standstill. Two barges carrying a combined 1 million gallons of heating fuel got stuck, one at the mouth of the Wicomico River and the other at the mouth of the Nanticoke River. Government officials issued dire warnings about the imminent need to ration supplies of home heating fuel. Those fears never came to fruition, but it was the first time anyone on the Eastern Shore had thought about fuel rationing since World War II.

President Jimmy Carter declared a state of emergency for the area in a nationally televised address in which he famously wore a casual cardigan while urging everyday Americans to turn down their thermostats. The hit television series *Roots* aired in January of 1977—folks watched it with multiple blankets piled atop their laps.

Winter Wonderland

The ice skating in that famous Bob Grieser photo wasn't the only type of fun the locals engaged in during the deep freeze. In St. Michaels the yacht-racing crowd on the Miles River got busy attaching gliders to their boats and conducting hastily planned ice races. Writing in the "Beautiful Swimmers" blog of the Chesapeake Bay Maritime Museum, Ken Noble recalled a magical day in Chestertown, Md. when he and a friend "skated from High Street to Quaker Neck Landing and back—about 13 miles down" the Chester River. He marveled:

We could very well have skated to Baltimore!

The freeze left Smith Islanders out of touch with civilization for nine long weeks. They did catch a bit of a break when, on orders from Governor Marvin Mandel, the state had essentials flown in by helicopter. Captain Eddie Somers, a native Smith Islander, put the deep freeze in perspective this way:

It seems like each generation of watermen has a benchmark winter that stands out to them. For my dad, it was 1936. For my grandfather, it was sometime in the teens. For me, it was 1977. That was the worst ice I've seen. No one was working.

Watermen up and down the Shore found themselves in the same bind. With hundreds of workboats idled, seafood processing houses had to shut down for lack of oysters. Thousands of people flocked to unemployment offices in search of temporary benefits. Oyster prices soared to a then-unprecedented $10 a bushel.

But watermen are a resourceful breed. Soon, some of them started operating in the manner of Inuit hunters up in the Arctic, or Minnesota fishermen. They hauled out chain saws to cut holes in the ice and commenced hand tonging. In order to get their catch to shore, they had to buy up just about every child's sled in stock at stores all over the Eastern Shore.

You Wouldn't Believe!

In Sussex County, Del., residents took it upon themselves to venture out on missions of mercy to feed the large numbers of waterfowl who were unable to feed on frozen farm fields. At one point, the state's chief biologist trucked half a ton of corn into the Indian River area near Bethany Beach.

There is one place today where you can get a first-hand look at the impact of the deep freeze, though you'll need a boat to get there. The combination of strong tides and heavy ice tilted Sharps Island Light (near Tilghman Island, Md.) by an angle of 15 degrees. Folks back then were sure that the light was going to topple over before the freeze came to a close.

It's the only caisson-style beacon in the Chesapeake Bay to ever suffer that kind of damage. After the thaw experts replaced the old glass lens with a new plastic one that was mounted on a leveling plate to compensate for the strange angle. Yup, it's still tilted out there—our own Eastern Shore Leaning Tower of Pisa.

Jessie Marsh was a 12-year-old boy living on Smith Island that winter. He would grow up to become an educator with Chesapeake Bay Foundation—a few years ago, he served up this vivid memory in a foundation newsletter:

This one morning we woke up, and there were these giant white walls on the whole west side of the island. The ice on the main part of the Bay had broken up in the wind, and the westerly winds had driven it into the shore. The ice had piled up, and they looked like icebergs, but they were actually ice piles. They were as high as 40 feet tall, walls of ice on the whole west side of the island.

Skating Down Memory Lane
Pretty much every year as winter arrives I post a little something on Facebook about the winter of 1977. It's such a rich memory

for so many folks. There is a story on the Secrets of the Eastern Shore website, too. In both places, people love sharing memories of the last great Eastern Shore deep freeze.

A few samples:

• **Janet Van Horn**: *I walked across the [Chesapeake] Bay that year!*

• **Terry Norville**: *OMG, people were driving cars on the ice!*

• **Maeve Finn**: *Being 16 at that time, all I have are fond memories of that winter. I lived on the Choptank River. Everything was frozen and white. You would step off the sea wall onto ice. Your private ice river! I would wear two coats, the second one a no-sleeve vest. All you had to do was open it up [the outer coat] like you were flashing someone and, BAM, you were off! So fast it felt as if you were flying. We got good at this. We learned to use the inner vest almost as if it were a rudder.*

• **Jon Abbott**: *I remember the hardship my parents and other watermen families endured that winter.*

• **Sue Haddox**: *Shhhh, don't tell my dad, but we did do-nuts on the ice in Ed's Mustang.*

• **A man calling himself "Major"**: *I've got pics of my old man and his friends seven miles off the Eastern Shore of Virginia, standing on twenty-foot-tall pressure ridges during that freeze.*

• **Susan Webster**: *That was the year the ocean froze at Ocean City. It was eerie standing on the beach and hearing nothing, no waves.*

• **Louise Windsor**: *It was about 13 weeks that the Deal Island Harbor was iced over, so bad that several boats broke apart from the pressure of the ice. I remember National Geographic came down and did a lot of photos, many aerial photos which were published in their magazine. It was a devastating time* *but so awesomely beautiful too.*

 • **Terri Pleasanton**: *I was 18 and dating a guy whose family was from Tangier Island. We took the mail boat over to attend a New Year's party that year. Long story short, we were stuck there for a week! I sat in the bathroom next to a kerosene heater reading a stack of National Geographics. After a week my mother hired a plane to pick us up. I'd never flown before, was scared to death. I remember looking down and seeing the Coast Guard cutters trying to get through.*

 • **Tina Swift**: *I remember that we still had to go to school!*

 • **Lenny Thomas Jr.**: *That's the freeze when I was 11 years old. I almost died. It was 30 mph winds. We skated out [such a long way, and] I tried to skate back. I was so cold. I was trying to fall asleep. I wanted to go to sleep. My buddy got home, and somebody rescued us.*

 • **Alice McJilton-Fox**: *I remember the Wicomico River being frozen solid that year. Coast Guard cutters had to come up and down the river to break up the ice so oil barges could get through. What a noise the ice made when it was breaking up, an eerie sound, especially during the middle of the night!*

 • **Patti Willis**: *I remember watermen were tonging out of the backs of pickup trucks parked on the Chesapeake Bay.*

THE GREATEST DAY IN THE HISTORY OF CHINCOTEAGUE GETS SWAMPED

Oh, the endless hours of preparation that must have gone into the celebration planned for Chincoteague, Va. on Nov. 15, 1922! Local newspapers promised it would mark "the beginning of a new era in the history" of a place that was even then renowned for its wild ponies and delectable seafood. Big-city papers on the western shore got into the act, too, billing it as the "biggest day in the island's history."

The pressure was on. The island's 3,500 residents were expecting up to 3,000 visitors. How many of those locals served on the various committees that planned parades and ceremonies and publicity and sporting events? How many families spruced up spare rooms to accommodate overnight guests? How many islanders prepared dishes for the big al fresco meal that would be served to all comers? Good lord, the governor was coming!

Washington (D.C.) Times, Oct. 19, 1922: *There has been no enterprise in the history of the Eastern Shore of Virginia that*

has created as much interest as the building of the system of
roads and bridges [stretching] from Chincoteague Island to the
mainland.

Who could have predicted that everything would turn to
muck and rain and wind, that the governor would go missing, that
all those hard-working islanders would fear he had died—and on
a day that was supposed to be such a grand showcase for their
hometown?

The Man with the Plan

From Native American days up through 1922, the only way to
get to Chincoteague Island was by water. The man who decided
to change that was John B. Whealton. Born into a storied Chincoteague family in 1860, Whealton didn't stay on the island once
he came of age. He went off to sea and visited the four corners of
the world. He became captain of his own schooner. He once spent
two days drifting in the Gulf of Mexico atop a wrecked vessel. He
worked on a lighthouse. He ran a shipwreck salvage company. He
became an engineer and learned about construction.

A North Carolina town hired him to manage its roads. He
built on that expertise after moving to Florida and taking an own-
ership stake in the Tampa Sand and Shell Company, which dealt
in the ingredients used to make roads that were as close as things
got back then to "paved."

Most of us know folks who have taken on big "retire-
ment" projects late in life, trying to contribute something to the
world before their time runs out. Whealton was nearing the mile-
stone age of 60 when he decided to put his expertise to use on
behalf of his childhood home. He would build a four-mile-long
road that would link Chincoteague to the mainland. As a toll road,
the project would eventually pay for itself and then turn a profit.

His concept quickly won civic support. The Virginia legislature approved the plan in 1919. When Whealton sought investors, it took him one short month to sell 70 percent of the stock available in his new company, which then proceeded to submit the lowest bid to the state in the amount of $144,000.

Whealton moved back home, taking up residence in a building on Main Street that in more recent decades served as the longtime home of Muller's Ice Cream Parlor. Construction work began on March 1, 1920.

Waylaid by Fire and Storms

Everyone saw that Whealton's road would bring big, profitable changes to Chincoteague. The place would be more accessible to visitors eager to see those wild ponies and sample those famous seafood dishes. The island's fish and oyster processors would have new, easier access to big-city markets by way of truck access to a mainland railroad line.

The *Washington Times*, Oct. 19: *The new road will be the greatest boon for Chincoteague of any project that has ever been undertaken in its history.*

The road was quite an engineering feat. A canal was dug out alongside the proposed route so that boat-borne crews and supplies could access the construction area. Humongous "mud-digger" machines scooped up muck from here and there, then dropped that muck inside of pilings sunk into the marsh. Multiple layers of oyster shells went atop that mud. Heavy rollers packed those shells down. More mud went atop the shell layers.

Six separate bridges would be built to carry the roadway over the various creeks, sounds, and narrows between Chincoteague and the mainland. One of those bridges would have a new-fangled kind of drawbridge to let boats through.

You Wouldn't Believe!

The Accomac, Va. *Peninsula Enterprise*, Nov. 11: *This roadway is about 50 feet wide and is several feet higher than the mark of the highest tides. ... When [the top layer of mud] dries out, [it] will leave a smooth, hard road.*

Getting to that point took longer than expected. In September of 1920, fire tore through downtown Chincoteague, destroying much of the Main Street area where the roadway was supposed to enter the island. Work on the road stopped. It was all hands on deck, clearing rubble and rebuilding. (A good number of the buildings that stand today on the island side of the causeway date to those frantic days.)

Work on the roadway resumed the following spring. But then the winter of 1921-22 brought a run of horrible weather, including one storm that swept away a partially built bridge over a stretch of water called Queen Sound.

Work finally drew to a close in the fall of 1922. Opening day festivities were set for Nov. 15. According to the historian Kirk Mariner in his excellent *Once Upon an Island: The History of Chincoteague*, the first man to cross to Chincoteague without a boat was an unauthorized pedestrian, W.W. Wood. A store clerk from the mainland town of Wattsville, he struck out across the causeway on his own authority on Sunday, Oct. 8.

More from Mariner: *Upon his arrival, islanders Daniel Jeffries and John Taylor, not to be outdone by a mainlander, started immediately in the opposite direction [on foot] to make the first recorded passage from the island to the mainland. Before the month was out Mrs. Edgar Twyford had proven that a woman, also, could [walk the route].*

The first vehicle across was a Buick driven by John B. Whealton himself. The final cost of $160,000 was only $16,000 more than Whealton's original estimate—not bad, considering all the delays and complications.

Across the Great Divide

The big day dawned at last. Cars streamed across the causeway. By 10 a.m., the streets of Chincoteague were "alive with visitors." When Governor E. Lee Trinkle and State Sen. George Walter Mapp arrived on the mainland side of the causeway, they were met by a welcoming committee of VIP citizens on horseback, who escorted them to the island.

The parade was spectacular. The *Worcester Democrat and Ledger Enterprise* newspaper reported that it began with marching veterans of World War I, who were followed by horseback riders in "gala attire," including a good number of "very attractive maidens riding the celebrated Chincoteague ponies." A marching band from Onancock performed. Floats with elaborate historical tableaux paid tribute to three founding families of islanders—the Whealtons (who dated their history to 1775), the Jesters (1780), and the Watsons (1790). Another float took the form of a duck blind. Uncle Sam rode the streets on a charger. Happy groups of schoolchildren "emitted all of the 95 percent of noise, of which, scientists say, a child is composed." They were followed by the firefighters who had done their level best the previous year to contain that horrible conflagration in downtown Chincoteague.

Once the parade ran its course, everyone walked over to a nearby field where the local high school football team faced off against their rivals from Onancock. The plan called for celebratory speechifying to come after that, followed in turn by that massive al fresco meal (served for a "reasonable" fee) and then a run of evening music, parties, and other entertaining diversions.

Hard Rain's a-Gonna Fall

Perhaps if weather forecasting had been better in those days, the events of Nov. 15, 1922 would have been called off and re-scheduled. The rain started falling in mid-afternoon, just as Gov. Trinkle started talking. When that drizzle turned into a downpour, the governor and his fellow speakers were moved inside a school building.

Some smart visitors sensed what was coming. Even in the dry weather of that morning, the parade of cars crossing the causeway for the first time had cut noticeable ruts into the still-soft mud atop the roadway. What was supposed to be a two-lane road had shrunk to a single lane even before the festivities began. Folks who made an early departure succeeded in getting across, but those who stayed had to endure quite an ordeal.

The *Worcester Democrat and Ledger Enterprise*, Nov. 18: *And thus we have to chronicle a rather distressing finale to an otherwise successful day. Parts of the highway from the mainland to the Island are constructed of marsh mud thrown up between barriers driven to hold it. This material had not sufficiently dried out to stand the amount of traffic to which it was subjected.*

The *Snow Hill Democratic Messenger*, Nov. 18: *The road, which earlier in the day had been an inviting expanse of shells, had been converted by the downpour of rain into a quagmire of mud.*

Cars started getting stuck at about 3:30 p.m. Their number grew into dozens of cars, which then turned into nearly a hundred. The blockade stretched "almost from the Mainland to the Island." With vehicles mired "up to their axles," drivers "could neither advance nor return."

Then as now, islanders tend to be a resourceful bunch. They ventured out into the mess, trying to help, but neither "man power" nor "mule power" succeeded in easing the logjam. Next, they sent fishing boats along the construction canal to rescue women and children.

The *Baltimore Sun*, Nov. 16: *The men, however, were preparing to spend the rest of the night in their cars, ... rain-soaked and cold.*

Rain kept falling in torrents. The wind picked up. The temperature dropped. Many cars built in those days were not exactly water-tight. More rescue boats arrived alongside the roadway, bringing as many blankets as locals were able to round up.

The *Worcester Democrat and Ledger Enterprise*, Nov. 18: *The morning found many cars still on the road; their occupants wearied, sick, and sore.*

A Governor Gone Missing

The governor's car was among those that got stuck. He was soon shepherded with his entourage onto a fishing boat.

The *Baltimore Sun*, Nov. 16: *Gov. E. Lee Trinkle was reported missing on one of the Virginia fishery boats earlier in the evening, [causing] quite a stir here.*

Under ordinary circumstances, that boat would have arrived on the mainland in less than an hour. But that hour passed, followed by another, and then a third.

More from the *Sun: In the three-hour interim after the Governor's departure people on this island and the mainland were frantically telephoning to points up and down the mainland, in an effort to get some word of the boat. Nobody had seen anything of her, and as it was dark and stormy, considerable apprehension was felt.*

Finally, a smidgeon of good news in that miserable night: Word got back to Chincoteague that after hours of bucking headwinds and waves, the boat carrying the governor had "staggered" into the harbor at "Wishard Point, near Locato."

The Day After, and Beyond

Some media reports in the aftermath of the disaster went over the top. The *Washington (D.C.) Herald* claimed that 500 cars were stranded. A more diligent source, historian Kirk Mariner, puts the actual number at precisely 96. When the rain finally stopped, islanders got back to rescuing their guests. They brought farm tractors, mules, and horses to bear on the problem. Every car was cleared from the causeway before the next day was out. There were no fatalities. Nor did I come across reports of serious illness or injury.

The *Worcester Democrat and Ledger Enterprise*, Nov. 18: *It is regretted that the day ended as it did, but Chincoteague is to be congratulated upon the enterprise of its public-spirited citizen, J.B. Whealton; and everyone hopes and believes that the stupendous engineering feat initiated mainly by him will be brought to a successful issue.*

That's pretty much what happened. Two short weeks later, daily traffic atop that causeway was numbering between 150 and 200 cars and trucks. Toll revenues were coming in at a rate of about $100 a day. The causeway cleared its construction debt and started turning a profit by 1928, in six short years.

The man behind the project, John B. Whealton, died that same year things turned profitable—he had moved back to Florida once the causeway was clear of trouble.

The road's profitable stretch was brief, however. Islanders started complaining loudly about paying those tolls, and the state responded by agreeing to take over the road from the toll company. Tolls were eliminated altogether by 1930. There would still be challenges ahead—the state had to rebuild some bridges after a big storm in 1936. A lot more work has happened in recent decades, including the replacement of every bridge along the causeway. As of this writing, all six structures are less than 30 years old.

Somewhere along the way, the causeway was given a formal name that honors its builder. Visitors to Chincoteague nowadays arrive along the John B. Whealton Memorial Causeway.

You Wouldn't Believe!

FOLKLORE!

THE WATERMAN CHANNELS A GREEK POET

The scene unfolded in waterfront town after waterfront town back in the 1960s. Local watermen gathered on benches, perhaps set around a pot-bellied stove. The smell of coffee and cigarettes filled the room. Someone started in telling a story.

Folklorist George Carey wandered the Delmarva Peninsula during the 1960s in search of scenes like that. He recorded many of the stories locals told and the legends they shared. Here is one such story he reprinted in his book, *A Faraway Place and Time: Lore of the Eastern Shore:*

When I was to the store the other day, there was an old fella sitting out in front smoking his pipe. He'd followed the water all his life and made his living oystering, crabbing and fishing. Just as I came in I heard him say:

"I've lived here all my life, and I've worked on the water and I'm getting kind of sick of it all. When I retire I'm gonna get me a rowboat and oar down the river. I'm gonna go and go until somebody asks me what that is I've got in my hand.

"Then I'll say, 'You don't know what an oar is?'

192

You Wouldn't Believe!

"And if he says 'No,' I'm gonna throw my oars away and let that rowboat go with the tide, and then I'm gonna spend the rest of my life right there."

It's All Greek to Him

Watermen are a cultural treasure on the Chesapeake and Delaware bays. They have been admired over the centuries for many qualities—their work ethic, their ingenuity, their wry sense of humor, and their deep connection with nature. One thing they are *not* generally known for, however, is a deep knowledge of classical Greek poetry.

But that story Carey heard comes straight out of Homer. Written nearly 3,000 years ago, the *Odyssey* tells the tale of a seafarer's long and difficult journey home after the Trojan war. Along the way, he encounters monsters and sirens and gods. He even pays a visit to the Underworld, where he asks a ghost for advice on bringing his long and arduous journey home to an end at last. Here is what that ghost says:

... then you must take up your well-shaped oar and go on a journey until you come where there are men living who know nothing of the sea, and who eat food that is not mixed with salt, who never have known ships whose cheeks are painted purple, who never have known well-shaped oars, which act for ships as wings do.

...

When, as you walk, some other wayfarer happens to meet you and says, "You carry a winnow fan on your bright shoulder," then you must plant your well-shaped oar in the ground, and render ceremonious sacrifice to the lord Poseidon.

You Wouldn't Believe!

That winnowing-fan business—in Homer's time, it was an oar-shaped farm implement used to separate wheat from chaff—adds up to the same thing that old waterman had talked about, longing to reach a place where he could put the hardships of making a living on the water behind him at last.

The Meandering Wonders of Folklore

What a circuitous route this passage in *The Odyssey* must have taken on its way to a bull session at a general store on Delmarva in the 1960s! Folklore is like that sometimes, with echoes sounding across oceans, centuries, languages, and cultures.

The writer Jan Harold Brunvand enjoyed a long, successful career collecting urban legends into books. His best-known tome is *The Vanishing Hitchhiker: American Urban Legends and Their Meanings.*

In a 1992 newspaper column, Brunvand recalled a day when he was traveling through Indiana during a snowstorm. He stopped at a gas station in a small town and got to chatting with the station's owner about the weather. The owner chimed in with this tale:

There was a guy around here one time who got really sick of the long, cold winters and the snow. One day he tied a snow shovel on the front of his truck, and he said he was going to drive south until someone asked him what that thing was. That's where he wanted to settle down.

Another twist to the Homeric tale of that "winnowing oar" comes by way of a legendary figure in the folklore field, Richard M. Dorson. He was doing research along the coast of Maine in the 1950s when he heard a tale about a young fisherman who set out to marry a girl who knew nothing about the sea:

So he went courting with a small carved model oar stuck

194

in his pocket. He decided to marry a girl who said she thought the oar was a "pudding stick."

He found such a girl, eventually, but the story does not have a happy ending, as it turns out the girl was a liar:

During their honeymoon his bride betrayed herself by using nautical terminology, saying, "There's been a squall, and I've got everything clewed up!"

Postscript: Here an Oar, There an Oar, Everywhere …
Brunvard shared one more version of Homer's "winnowing oar" in that newspaper column, this one played for laughs. As the discipline of folklore studies took off in the mid-1900s, the oar story popped up in so many places and in so many versions that it became an inside joke among academics in the field.

When John Greenway retired from his post as editor of the *Journal of American Folklore* in 1968, he included this bit of whimsy in his letter of farewell, amid a section in which he confesses to having grown tired of navigating the controversies and in-fighting of academia:

Your Editor now proposes to throw [the famed folklorist] Dr. Richard M. Dorson across his shoulder and walk steadily inland until someone asks him what that thing [on his shoulder] is. There he will lay down his burden and settle in peace forever.

CHEESE IN YOUR COFFEE?

I went to see a talk a few years back put on by a little nonprofit group called the South Dorchester Folk Museum. The woman up on stage shared sweet memories that night about old-time country stores in the remote corners of Dorchester County, Md.

The room was full of local old-timers. At the end of the talk, one old guy raised his hand and asked whether everyone else remembered the big "wheels" of cheese that used to be displayed prominently in those stores. Then he said:

Because, as we all know, people in [the town of] Crocheron like to put cheese in their coffee.

The old-timers in the audience all laughed knowingly. I had never heard of this coffee-and-cheese business. I tried every which way to research the topic online, but came up mostly empty.

Fortunately, I had another place to turn. I threw the question out to the Secrets of the Eastern Shore community on Facebook. Whoo-boy, did I get an education! Nearly 300 comments rolled in. I'm highlighting some here. (FYI, the comments mentioning how you should never use grated cheese are responding to the fact that I had put up a photo of my ignorant self scooping grated cheese into a coffee cup with a quizzical look on my face.)

Sherri Anthony: *I was told once on a visit to Smith Island, Md. ... [that] a lot of fishermen would take cold toast out with them. They would pour hot coffee from their thermos and put cheese in it. It would float on top and melt and then they could spread it on their toast to eat on a chilly morning.*

Deborah Jones: *My dad put cheese in his coffee all the time. He used cheddar cheese. Chunks in his coffee, then let it melt. Bring it out with a fork. Put the cheese on a biscuit. Drink the coffee the way you like it, oil and all. Enjoy!*

Christine Todd-Barlow: *JIM, PLEASE DON'T GRATE THE CHEESE FOR CHEESE AND COFFEE!!!*

Mary Spellman Handley: *My stepfather was from [the town of] Bishops Head [in Dorchester County]. Before he married my mom, we would visit him. He would wake us up for breakfast. He would cut big chunks of cheddar cheese (not shredded) for the coffee. Also on the menu was a black agate roaster pan with a giant rockfish in it, smothered in tomatoes. For breakfast! I was nine. We were from Baltimore. We ended up staying.*

Kimberly Landon Meyer: *My grandfather used to do this. But he put the cheese in first so the hot coffee would melt the cheese. Then he would scoop the melted cheese onto toast. He was from Virginia's Eastern Shore.*

Julie Laird: *My grandmother, a Smith Islander, always put sharp cheddar cheese in her coffee. After she drank the coffee she spooned out the cheese and ate it on crackers. Lots of Smith Islanders did it and still do. Yummy.*

Martha Middleton Simpson: *I live in Accomack County, Va. I remember as a child that my mother's cousin would do this for me, usually on a Sunday evening. He put the cheese on homemade biscuits after it melted. This was in the 1950s. Great* *memory!*

Heidi Coleman Glasgow: *The late, great Ray O. Moore from Toddville, Md. taught me this. He said not to cut the cheese but to break pieces off. He said if you cut it then it wouldn't melt as well. His favorite was Colby in instant Maxwell House. We all liked it. Yum.*

Jane Phillips: *My grandmother who passed in 2014 at the age of 104 used to do this for me when I was little. She used longhorn for me but she used sharp [cheddar] for herself. Loved it!!! And her. Miss you, MomMom!*

Jinx Pich Banks: *My father-in-law always did this, then spread it on bread or biscuits. He was from Pittsville, Md. He put small chunks of sharp cheese in a cup. Poured hot coffee. Put a saucer on top of the cup. After a few minutes, spread the cheese.*

Amber McGinnis: *I had it as a treat when I was a kid in Toddville, Md. The coffee was instant with cream and sugar. [We would put the cheese] on saltines.*

Deborah Gootee: *Yep, my grandfather from Bruceville in Talbot County, Md. let us young grandkids have coffee and cheese with him for breakfast. Chunks of sharp cheddar dipped in coffee to soften and then pop in your mouth. Almost as good as our ice cream "parties" with Dixie cups from Olin Whitley's store.*

Linda Phillips: *My great grandfather from Delmar, Md. would put chunks of cheese in his coffee and spoon it out to my siblings and me as a treat when we visited. I can still see him sitting at the dining table with the six of us gathered around, waiting for our turn to get the cheese off his spoon. It has always been my best memory of him.*

Maggie Glidden: *My grandparents and parents bought the wheel of cheese at Sam Jones's store in Church Creek, Md. Cut [the cheese] into small chunks with hot perked coffee over*

*it and then put [the melted cheese] on hot homemade biscuits,
sometimes sweet potato biscuits.*

Janice Marshall: *We still do [this] on Smith Island, Md.
The coffee tastes so much better when the cheese melts, and the
grease rises to the top of the coffee. The milk fat in the cheese
makes the coffee taste so good. [In the days before my watermen
husband] Bobby passed away, he didn't have any appetite. The
only things he wanted were clam chowder and cheese and coffee.*

L Stella Durango: *I'm finding this interesting because my
mom would also drop cheese into her coffee, and we both know
she wasn't from anywhere near Dorchester. (Note: Stella is my
sister-in-law—her family's roots are in Colombia, South America.)*

Autumn Sonne: *How interesting. This is a typical Sami
tradition mostly found in Finland and Sweden. I wonder who
brought the tradition here to the Shore originally?*

Of Kaffeost and Juustolepä

Those last two comments hint at what might be the truth here—
namely, that this tradition goes way back through the centuries
and pops up nowadays in various interesting ways and out-of-
the-way places. The Sami people of Scandinavia have a special
name for coffee and cheese—*kaffeost*. The preferred cheese in
that delicacy, *juustoleipä*, is sometimes known on these shores as
"Finnish squeaky cheese." But be warned: The version you might
find online or in specialty stores is probably made from cow's
milk. The real authentic stuff is made from reindeer's milk.

One other connection makes that Swedish turn interesting: The Swedes, of course, were the first Europeans to settle in
Delaware, arriving in what's now the Wilmington area way back
in 1638. That colony didn't last long, but many Swedes remained

in that area through the Dutch, British, and American eras of the centuries that followed.

When it comes to that Colombia comment from my sister-in-law, well, I laughed out loud upon seeing the first relevant headline in an internet search: "Weird Things That Exist Only in Colombia." Many Colombian coffee shops today include *café con queso* on the menu. Just like folks on Smith Island and in remote Crocheron, they like to spoon the gooey cheese out of their coffee and onto bread for breakfast.

Maybe someday an enterprising culinary historian will get to the bottom of where this tradition first took shape. Hopefully, that historian will also figure out how cheese 'n' coffee traveled to various little corners of the world and how it is folks in each of those corners ended up regarding it as a one-of-the-kind local treasure.

GIRLS ARE BAD LUCK ON NEW YEAR'S DAY

I first learned about this strange tradition on the Secrets of the Eastern Shore Facebook page, thanks to a man named Kevin Cusick who posed this question to the community on New Year's Day, 2017:

When I was little MomMom used to wake me up early on New Year's morning and send me on my way to all the windows in the neighborhood. Apparently, if a little boy was the first person to wish them happy New Year they would have good luck for the year and in return they all reached into their purses and gave me change. I've not found one other person my own age who ever did that, but I lived in a neighborhood of old-timers. Has anyone else from Chincoteague [Island, Va.] heard of this tradition?

Quite a few others soon chimed in with similar memories. A sampling:

Beth Messick: *I'm from Salisbury, Md., not Chincoteague, but I do remember that it was forbidden for a female to be the first one in the door on New Year's Day.*

Christine: *Growing up in [the towns of] Cambridge and*

201

Secretary, Md. I was always told that a male was supposed to be the first to enter your home on New Year's Day if you wanted to avoid bad luck all year.

Liza: *When I was a child on Hooper's Island, my older sister's husband always visited the neighbors on New Year's Day so that a dark-haired man would be first in the door! And black-eyed peas were the traditional food, said to bring wealth in the new year.*

Pamela Foley: *As a girl growing up on Chincoteague, I was always jealous of the little boys who came [to our door and received] change on New Year's Day. My mom would call across the street for the neighbor's boy to come over for [his] change. I never knew why until now. Thanks!*

Barbara Smalling: *I was born and raised in Somerset County, in Fairmount, Md. I remember how, on January 1, Mr. Bankshire "Banks" Waters would be the first visitor to everyone's home. He always wore a fur parka with a hood. He looked like an Eskimo! We children loved to see him come because he arrived with lots of brown bags of goodies: apples, oranges, nuts, and hard candy. After his arrival, we girls would be allowed to go outside of the house. However, we were not allowed to visit anyone because we were told that it would bring "bad luck" to the families we visited.*

The Forgetfulness of Mabel Parks

In jumping down this rabbit hole, I found my way to a tradition folklorists refer to as "first-foot," a reference to the first person across the threshold in a new year. It was big in Wales and the north of England in centuries gone by, and remains popular there today. The key distinction over there isn't so much gender. Rather, it's between dark-haired good luck and light-haired bad luck.

You Wouldn't Believe!

The dark-haired good luck charms are supposed to bring symbolic gifts, like chunks of coal to go in the family hearth.

Folklorist Donna Heddle once speculated that the dark/light distinction might go back to the days when families in England and Wales were at risk of deadly raids by violent, light-haired Vikings. Other versions of the first-foot superstition have been traced to Serbia, Sweden, Greece, and the country of Georgia.

The late Tom Flowers–aka "The Old Honker"—was a famous storyteller from Dorchester County, Md. whose tales are collected in an out-of-print 1998 book, *Shore Folklore: Growing Up with Ghosts, 'N Legends, 'N Tales, 'N Home Remedies.*

Flowers grew up on Hoopers Island at a time—the late 1920s and early 1930s—when this legend was taken very, very seriously, so much so, he writes, that "pots of scalding water sat on the stoves for ... a visitor" of the wrong gender. One of his stories focuses on a forgetful young woman. Apparently, the strict "first-foot" rules on Hoopers in those days applied not just to crossing the threshold of a home, but to stepping over a property line in the yard.

Mabel Parks forgot herself, completely forgot what day of the week it was, but more importantly forgot that it was New Year's Day when she went to her neighbor's well to draw water, but Evelyn Ruark had seen her and was deeply upset to think that Mabel would break such a well-kept tradition.

When Mabel did remember it later in the day, she just hoped that no one had seen her. It would be hard to get through the night without knowing. She would know the very first thing the next morning. As soon as it was light, she made her way to her good friend, Evie Ruark's. The door was latched. She had been seen.

You Wouldn't Believe!

The Ruarks blamed all their bad luck on Mabel's visit. They would not speak to her, but they let the community know that she was the cause of their problems. When [a family member,] Jane Ruark, died suddenly, they openly blamed [Mabel] and categorized her as an evil witch.

It is sad to report that the community sided with the Ruarks. They gave no sympathy to Mabel. She and her family were ostracized.

I could remember at least ten years of the argument. I must say that as a child, I always felt sorry for Miss Mabel—but ... there were no "ifs, ands, or buts" for my father to accept any reason for a woman visiting another house on New Year's Day.

Flowers notes that the rules were eased up a little bit as the years passed. In later times, women were allowed to visit on New Year's Day, but only if a boy or man had come calling first.

A Pair of Postscripts

First, a woman named Betty Parks provided the laugh-out-loud comment in all the back-and-forth when she said:

In 1977 the first visitor to my house was a single, dark hair, male. I married him later that year.

Second, Laura Davis from Chincoteague Island chimed in with the news that this tradition is still alive and well on that Virginia island:

My mother-in-law does this. We take our boys out to the neighbors' houses now!

You Wouldn't Believe!

CHARACTERS!

A 'DEGENERATE' ON BOLINGBROKE CREEK

Sometimes magic happens when you're shopping for a new home. You just "know," instinctively, that you've found the right place. That's what happened in 1959 for one couple looking to relocate in Talbot County, Md.

I asked this real estater what the natives did in these parts. He said, "We don't do nothing but go crabbing and drink." I knew he was telling the truth because right after he said that he fell on his ear. Man, he was stoned!' I said, "This is it! We'll dig it here."

That is from a biography of a Hollywood star titled Robert Mitchum: *Baby, I Don't Care*, by Lee Server. Mitchum and his wife did indeed seal that deal on a waterfront farm along Bolingbroke Creek, not far from the town of Trappe.

'They Thought I Was Some Kind of Degenerate'
Both Mitchum and the former Dorothy Spence had spent childhood time on the Delmarva Peninsula. Mitchum's early life was an itinerant affair. Most newspaper mentions of his 1917 birth put

that event in Bridgeport, Conn. though one odd outlier of a story says it happened in Elkton, Md.

Mitchum was the son of a railroad man, but he never got to know his father. He was just two years old when the elder Mitchum died in an accident while coupling and uncoupling freight cars. The family was living in Charlestown, S.C. at the time.

In the aftermath of that tragedy, Mitchum and a younger brother ended up living with their grandparents on a farm in Felton, Del. Mitchum stayed there into his teenage years. Much later, after he had become famous the world over as a Hollywood tough guy, newspaper reporters had fun nosing around Felton in search of old memories.

Miss Roberta S. Cornelius taught algebra and geometry to Mitchum in 9th grade.

Yes, I remember. ... He sat near a window, the second desk from the back, where he could look out and dream ... a dreamer with his eyes half-closed.

Mitchum was not what you'd call a star student. Miss Cornelius tried and tried to get her young dreamer of a pupil to realize that he would never succeed in life unless he studied more and worked harder. She also recalled:

One day he and a boy, who turned out later to be a preacher, took out to hitchhike and ended up in Connecticut.

Mitchum got expelled from the local Felton School. The only description of his offense that I have come across is that he did "something in the girls' dressing room." There is no indication of what—or how bad—that "something" might have been. A farmer and former classmate named Gardner Hersey described Mitchum as "an ornery boy, but a good one," who generally got into the "kind of mischief that you overlook, that's all."

Another former classmate said: "If he hadn't become a

movie star, he was the kind of boy I would have forgotten."

After his expulsion Mitchum ended up at Caesar Rodney High School in nearby Camden. That's where he met his future bride, Dorothy Spence. That's also where Mitchum became a high school dropout. He started hopping freight trains to wander the country at the age of 14.

In later life, he summed up his time in Fenton and Camden this way:

They thought I was some kind of degenerate. They ran me out of town so many times that it finally took.

From Flat Broke to Hollywood Legend

At about 16, Mitchum was arrested for vagrancy in Georgia and sentenced to work on a chain gang. He promptly escaped. Somewhere in the years that followed he did time as a ditch digger for the Civilian Conservation Corps. He worked in mining and manufacturing, too. Somehow, in 1935, he reunited with a former high school classmate, Dorothy Spence. They soon got married.

The Mitchums found their way to California in the early 1940s. Robert was in his mid-20s. He arrived carrying his life savings of $26 in his pocket. He had a sister there, and she's the one who suggested he join a local theater troupe.

One thing led to another. His first movie role came in the 1943 western *Border Patrol*. Two years later, he was nominated for an Academy Award for a supporting role in *The Story of G.I. Joe*. Soon, he was starring opposite Jane Russell, Marilyn Monroe, Rita Hayworth, and other A-list stars. Among his most famous films are *The Night of the Hunter, The Sundowners*, and *Cape Fear*. Today, the American Film Institute ranks him #23 in a list of the 50 greatest screen legends of all time.

'All True—Booze, Brawls, Broads, All True'

Legends abound when it comes to Robert Mitchum. Most of those tales involve booze and broads. Mitchum enjoyed being a man with a dicey reputation, judging by a comment he once made to a journalist:

[The stories about me are] all true–booze, brawls, broads, all true. Make up some more if you want.

He was arrested at least once during his Hollywood years, on a "narcotics" charge. That might sound big and scary, but it was actually a simple matter of Mitchum smoking pot with a couple of actresses.

Another in the endless parade of Mitchum rumors is that the decision to move away from California was his wife's idea—supposedly, she was sick of his affairs. Whatever the case, the Mitchums bought Belmont Farm for $140,000. That 200-plus acre affair sits along wide Bolingbroke Creek, near where Route 50 crosses the Choptank River. The main house was (and still is) an 1850 Georgian colonial with 12 rooms, topped by an octagonal cupola. It boasted two sun porches, two marble fireplaces, and a living room that stretched over two levels.

The Mitchums chose Trappe over a more remote and isolated alternative, on an island off of South Carolina. The Talbot County place didn't come cheap by the standards of those days, and the family paid more in Maryland taxes than they had in California, so the move wasn't about money. "Maryland isn't as remote" as the South Carolina alternative, Mitchum once said.

[But] I can fly anywhere in no time at all. When I'm there it's like being in a different world.

The Mitchums were no different than many of the new-comers landing on Delmarva nowadays. They wanted the best of both worlds—small towns and isolated countryside within easy striking distance of big cities and big airports.

Later, Mitchum would recall his Bolingbroke years as an idyllic time of "lost, nostalgic, splendid isolation." He still starred in pictures during these years—*The Longest Day, Cape Fear*, and *El Dorado* among them. But after the work was done, he'd return to the Eastern Shore and ... do nothing, mostly.

He never answered the phone. He had a boat but rarely fired it up. He loved fishing but never went. For days on end, he would "just goof, sit there, and stare" at the setting sun. He had newspapers delivered, but the only section he ever read was the comics. He once described the funny pages as "the only part [of the news] that changes."

This laid-back lifestyle was at the heart of his love for the farm and its surroundings:

My unsocial nature is well known. [On the Eastern Shore], I can be as unsocial as I want and nobody gives a damn.

His wife was the one who dealt with tenant farmers and hired laborers to plant and harvest soybeans and corn. The farm was financially self-sufficient, Mitchum said, unless you counted the liquor bills.

Ah, that. Rumors abound to this day about Mitchum's drinking. It's hard to separate fact from fiction when it comes to the local legends that involve a drunken, belligerent Hollywood star getting booted out of the Cambridge Yacht Club and the Tidewater Inn in Easton.

Many locals seemed to like Mitchum well enough. The security guard on his property described him as a "regular guy" who would often help out the hired hands by driving tractors and pitching hay. The Mitchums did a lot of landscaping, but that didn't go so well. Sightseers often dug up little trees and newly planted shrubs for keepsakes of their visit to the star's home. One old newspaper article indicates that Mitchum took even this in stride:

The actor himself greets the rubberneckers cordially, say-ing, he doesn't mind visitors, "but my children shoot at them."

Mitchum eventually found his farmland passion: raising horses. At one point, he had more than 20 of them at Belmont Farm. He would enter them in races, rodeos, and other events. Mitchum's daughter, Petrine, moved to Trappe at the age of 8 and lived there until she was 15.

My fondest memories of Belmont are riding my horses through the woods and along the dirt road from Chancellor Point to the next road over," she once said. "It was a long sandy road through the forest on which we could gallop. Also, I loved swim-ming with my horses in the creek. It was so wonderful living right on the waterfront and being able to go crabbing off the pier.

By all accounts then, the seven years the Mitchums spent on the Eastern Shore were an idyllic time. They returned to full-time California living in 1966, for reasons that are shrouded in typical Mitchum mysteriousness, with the rumor mill saying that his wife found out about her husband's affair with actress Shirley MacLaine. She apparently wanted to be out west at all times so as to keep a closer eye on him while he was working in Hollywood.

Robert Mitchum died in 1997, at the age of 79. If you're ever tempted to move away from this area, you might want to keep another quote of his in mind:

The biggest mistake in my life was selling my Eastern Shore property.

Postscript: The Quote Machine
As you can tell, Robert Mitchum was quite the quotable guy. A few more, just for fun:

You Wouldn't Believe!

• *These kids only want to talk about acting method and motivation. In my day all we talked about was screwing and overtime.*

• *There just isn't any pleasing some people. The trick is to stop trying.*

• *You know what the average Robert Mitchum fan is? He's full of warts and dandruff and he's probably got a hernia too, but he sees me up there on the screen and he thinks if that bum can make it, I can be president.*

• *They think I don't know my lines. That's not true. I'm just too drunk to say 'em.*

• *Got the same attitude I had when I started. Haven't changed anything but my underwear. I've played everything except midgets and women. People can't make up their minds whether I'm the greatest actor in the world - or the worst. Matter of fact, neither can I.*

If you are interested in reading more of the local legends that still linger on the Eastern Shore about Robert Mitchum—or about other Hollywood connections to our local landscape—check out *Stardust by the Bushel: Hollywood on the Chesapeake Bay's Eastern Shore*, by Brent Lewis. It was published late in 2021.

THE ADVENTURER WHO PASSED OUT AT FENWICK ISLAND

Facts are few and far between when it comes to the strange scene that unfolded at Fenwick Island, Del. on Christmas morning of 1931. But fuel for a fictional extravaganza? Now that's another story—one that has the potential to unfold along the lines of *The Odyssey, Moby Dick, Gulliver's Travels*, or *The Life of Pi*.

On Christmas morning, Fenwick Island Lighthouse keeper Charles L. Gray surveyed the horizon, just as he did every other morning. Off to the southeast he spied what looked like a small vessel out in the ocean, perhaps half a mile away. Was it lodged on a sandbar? Wait, was that a human body laying out there?

Alaska or Bust!?!?
Keeper Gray went to investigate. Yup, it was a sailboat. Yup, it was a body. The man was alive, but he had seemingly passed out. He was dressed strangely, his garments all thick with fur.

Gray loaded the man onto his boat and sailed back to shore. Over the next two days, he nursed the exhausted patient back to consciousness and health. During their time together, the man told Gray that he was an "Eskimo." (Nowadays, most folks prefer to use the word *Inuit*.) He told Gray that he hailed from Greenland, which is about 2,500 miles away. The journey from Fenwick Island to Las Vegas is comparable.

The man told Gray he was southbound, headed for the Panama Canal. Once through there, he planned to ride through the canal and sail up the Pacific Coast until he got to Alaska.

Wait, *what?* I did a rinky-dink web calculation on this—that's a voyage of 10,000 miles.

Keeper Gray wrote up this smidgeon of information and reported it to his superiors. He described the Inuit man's boat as small, so it's quite possible that it was a traditional umiak. The history of these vessels can be traced back to Siberia in the distant mists of human history. They were brought to North America by the Thule people, ancestors of the Inuit.

Umiaks tend to run about 30 feet long. They are made from a frame of driftwood or whalebone that's then wrapped in the stretched and dried skin of walruses or seals. The boats have an amphibious aspect, as Inuits would attach sled legs to the bottom and run them along the ice-covered land surfaces of the arctic.

Out on the sea, umiaks maneuver in primitive fashion. They don't have a keel, so our Fenwick Island visitor would not have been able to tack back and forth to catch stronger winds during his 10,000-mile marathon sail. It's possible that by 1931 this man was able to attach an outboard motor to his boat, but it seems a little early for that, especially for a man from remote Greenland. The lighthouse keeper made no mention of a motor.

Imagination Station
More than a dozen newspapers around the county published a

bare-bones, one-paragraph snippet about Gray's report of this strange visitor from the north. But the questions raised by that visitor's arrival on Fenwick Island remain unanswered. Why did he set out on such a journey? Was he just looking for adventure? Testing his endurance? Was there some more mundane purpose involved—a business situation? I dunno, a religious pilgrimage?

I looked for tales of this voyager in other newspapers along his route, but I came up empty. And so we end up right back where we started, fingers crossed that someone with a rich imagination will be inspired to take hold of this strange anecdote and turn it into a story. So again with the opening question: Any novelists out there?

FRUITLAND'S ACCIDENTAL AUCTIONEER

An earlier chapter here, "When Delaware Delivered the 'True Spirit of Christmas,'" tells the story of how the seasonal holly wreath industry took off in the late 1800s and early 1900s, starting in Southern Delaware and then moving into Maryland, where holly soon became known as "Maryland's Christmas Crop."

The unlikely mecca of that crop was the little town of Fruitland, just below Salisbury. A holly farm market started up there around World War I, but it got off to a slow and drab start. A few vendors had tables set up on a vacant lot near the fire hall. A few customers meandered around.

The man who changed that atmosphere was an Eastern Shore character of the first order, Hurvey Mezick. Here is how he dressed:

He wears a brown overcoat, indiscriminately splattered with soup and gravy, and a battered hat that is adorned with safety pins.

Here is the executive summary of his resume:

Mr. Mezick is a farmer, canning-house worker, and auc-

tioneer [who describes his various activities in life as] "a little of everything, not much of anything."

In the Spur of the Moment

Hurvey Mezick found himself wandering through that drab little holly market one day. Sales seemed slow. Everything was too quiet. He decided to take matters into his own hands:

While buyers were picking over the wreaths I just jumped up and shouted, "I bid five, I bid six, I bid 10, I bid 11 ... Are you done? Are you done? Sold!" ... I just felt moved that day.

Mezick sold a slew of holly with that stunt. Farmers started offering him a piece of their proceeds if he would perform his fast-talking schtick with their wreaths. Soon enough, the whole market was transformed, with Hurvey Mezick now at center stage. Customers gathered in front of a stage. Trucks rolled up one by one, taking their turn under the Mezick spotlight.

Every time he mentioned a new [price], one of the dealers indicated he would buy at that price by closing his eyes, nodding his head, or turning his cigar at a slight angle.

Mezick's flair for showmanship turned the Fruitland auction into a big hit. Every year, newspapers from near and far wrote stories about the town's colorful holly auction, which was the only one of its kind in the country. Those stories almost always told the tale of Hurvey Mezick, accidental auctioneer.

Trucks, cars, and jalopies of all descriptions line up for the sale day in the streets. ...

The Fruitland auction outlasted the man who put it on the map. Other auctioneers worked the market after Mezick's death in 1947. The event closed up shop once and for all in the late 1960s.

Deep in the Pocomoke Forest

Before winning fame as Fruitland's auctioneer, Mezick tried his own hand at the holly wreath game. That work would begin with holly-hunting journeys deep into the dense, swampy forests along the Pocomoke River and its tributaries. Here he is, remembering:

It sounds easy but it was a lot of work. You go into the swamp and you get interested in what you are doing. First thing you know you are lost. Sometimes it takes you three or four hours to cipher just how to get out. You always try to stay on high ground but before you know it you go swosh into the mud up to your knees or your waist. Then you try another way out and keep on trying till you make it.

One time, in a down year for berries, Mezick found a grove of spectacular holly, "flaming with red." He and his brother offered the landowner $210 for exclusive access.

That was the most beautiful holly I ever saw—long sprays of shiny leaves, thick with real red berries.

Mezick and his brother didn't make wreaths out of that holly. They spent all their time gathering twigs and branches, which they then sold to middlemen. Locals used to call that way of doing business "box holly." The brothers packed 500 boxes and sold them for $10 a box.

For two and a half weeks' work, that was a killing. After we paid expenses we got about $1K each.

THE MAN WHO MADE ICE CREAM TASTE BETTER

The only folks who screamed for ice cream when that delicacy first came on the market were the filthy rich. The history of the ice cream parlors we know today dates back to France in the late 1600s, but the sweet treat didn't take off with the general population until the arrival of industrial refrigeration technologies in the 1870s.

Even then, there were problems. Early parlors served ice cream on paper plates that were too flimsy to hold up. To make matters worse, the cheap disposable spoons they handed out were made of tin. They had sharp edges that could cut the tongue. Plus, tin had a metallic aftertaste that overwhelmed the flavors at hand.

The man who fixed these problems is a memorable character named John H. Mulholland. An Irish immigrant who roamed the Western Hemisphere in his younger years, Mulholland eventually found his way lower Delaware, settling first in Laurel and then in Milford.

Rudyard Kipling Wrote a Poem About Him

Born in Belfast in 1865, Mulholland moved to Canada as a teenager. He was in Montreal for a while, then joined the Royal Canadian Mounted Police, traveling here, there, and everywhere in the Great White North. His unit helped squash one of the last Indian rebellions in Saskatchewan. Mulholland earned a medal for his role in that campaign.

After leaving the Mounties, he returned to Ireland in 1887. He must have been broke because he paid his fare across the ocean by taking on the job of watching over a shipment of cattle in the cargo hold. The work did not go well. All hell broke loose down there when the cattle busted through their pens during a storm.

The writer Rudyard Kipling was a passenger on that ship. He turned that crazy incident into a poem titled "Mulholland's Contract." No need to look it up—I'll include those verses at the end here.

After surviving his cattle ordeal, Mulholland stayed in Ireland for a couple of years. He wanted to move to Philadelphia, but he couldn't make it work, so he settled in Toronto. There, in 1890, he married Emma Jean Harper. The couple managed to move to Philly soon thereafter. They had two sons, Harry and Frederick.

Mulholland was in the advertising game by this point, making signs to help promote businesses. One of his clients was a fledgling operation called Breyer's Ice Cream—William Breyer operated a handful of ice cream shops at this point, making deliveries by horse-drawn carriage. That company would eventually start cranking out ice cream in gallon containers. The brand lives on today, of course—it's now owned by corporate behemoth Unilever.

Mulholland's Ice Cream Adventures

The first ice cream parlor problem that Mulholland solved was those flimsy paper plates. Here, he found inspiration through his advertising and printing acumen. Small-fry ice cream makers were eager to step up their marketing game in the early 1900s, but they faced some sticky obstacles. If they printed advertising slogans on those flimsy plates, the ink would run while folks were still eating—not an appetizing prospect. Instead, they printed messages on the bottoms of plates, which failed to get much in the way of results because ... who turns a plate full of melted ice cream upside down?

Mulholland applied for his first patent in 1915. His idea was to print advertisements on the top side of the plate, then top it with a sturdy, transparent, waterproof piece of upper paper cut into the same shape. The two layers would be fused together with clear adhesive. The birth of today's lamination process didn't arrive until the 1930s, but he was working along that path.

From his patent application: *The purpose of my invention [is] to provide a perfectly sanitary dish or plate made of paper with printed matter of any color or any kind of advertising matter or any kind of ornamentation in colors, and have such printed matter or advertisement readily observable from the top or upper face of the plate where it will be most conspicuous.*

Mulholland really hit it big when he turned his attention a few years later to those tin spoons. His inspiration came in a visit to lower Delaware, which then ranked as quite the innovative place when it came to making wooden baskets for transporting fruits and vegetables. The basket-making innovation that caught Mulholland's attention involved the use of veneer in cheap baskets made of sweetgum wood during the fruit-drying process.

That wood had no taste at all. Delaware basket makers

were using it so as to protect the flavor of the produce. Mulholland was soon working with the A.W. Robinson Basket Company in Laurel to figure out a die-press method of cutting flat "spoons." A short time later, he set out to use the one-two punch of steam and pressure to "bend" the wood and give it a spoonish indentation deep enough to hold ice cream.

Mulholland had a notion that he was onto something big. He put his son Harry in charge of bringing the manufacturing process to the finish line while he headed out across the country on sales calls. His strategy involved showing up at ice cream companies with a "spoon in one pocket and a piece of sandpaper in the other."

Mulholland still had the marketing game in his blood. He chose the clever name of "Bentwood Spoons." But his early sales calls didn't go so well. Not only were the wooden spoons new and unfamiliar, but they were also more expensive than tin spoons. His big break came a couple of years later when the folks at the now fast-growing Breyer's Ice Cream decided to trust their former advertising guy and give both plates and spoons a try.

The Glory Years of J.H. Mulholland Co.
Through the decades that followed, J.H. Mulholland Company had corporate offices in Philadelphia while its primary manufacturing operations were in Milford. The Mulholland family had homes in both places. The one in Milford sat on the shores of Haven Lake. Once that Breyer's breakthrough happened, the business started to take off. But then disaster struck.

The *Wilmington Morning News*, Jan. 22, 1924: *Fire today destroyed the main building of the wooden spoon plant of J.H. Mulholland Company, entailing a loss estimated at $50,000. The building was a one-story corrugated iron structure and contained*

many valuable machines ... designed for special work in the
manufacture of the patented wooden spoon. This was the only fac-
tory of its kind in the country.

The night was cold and windy. A frozen water main cost
precious time, as firefighters had to regroup and send a pumping
engine down to the Mispillion River. One hundred Mulholland
Company workers lost their jobs that night.

Mulholland regrouped and rebuilt. He bought the former
Reis and Hirsch vegetable cannery at the north end of Marshall
Street, right on the Mispillion River.

In the big-picture scheme of things, Mulholland's timing was perfect. The automobile was coming into its own in the
1920s. Interest in road-tripping was through the roof. Refrigeration technologies kept improving, to the point where it became
easy as pie to keep product frozen in a cute little roadside spot.
Ice cream parlors started popping up everywhere.

To say that J.H. Mulholland Company became the second
biggest employer in Milford—with 200-plus employees—under-
states the firm's success. Needing more manufacturing capacity,
the company opened plants in Michigan, Maine, and Oregon.
They started making mustard paddles and lollypop sticks. They
moved into the medical market with tongue depressors.

Mulholland kept leading the company forward, growing the business by leaps and bounds even as the Depression
arrived. Alas, his wife Emma died young, in 1932. Perhaps this
had something to do with the family's announcement around this
time that Mulholland's son Harry would take over the business.
Harry would eventually become a state senator. His father would
marry for a second time, this time to a former Breyer's Ice Cream
employee named Marie Wimserberger.

The J.H. Mulholland company kept chugging along

through World War II. In the postwar years, however, innovations in the plastics industry changed everything. Plastic spoons that were both strong and cheap made wooden spoons obsolete. The Marshall Street facility shut down in the 1950s, as did the rest of the company's operations. In 1953, the Association of Ice Cream Manufacturers gave Mulholland a "Lifetime Achievement Award" in recognition of his company's accomplishments.

John Mulholland as Milford Civic Leader

There is one more aspect of the Mulholland story that needs to be noted here—and that involves the way his living arrangement was an early version of something quite common nowadays on the Delmarva Peninsula. In modern terminology, he would qualify as a "weekender" or "part-time resident," splitting his time between the big city and his place in the country.

When it came to issues of local citizenship, however, John Mulholland didn't act like a part-timer—especially with his beloved Haven Lake. He thought Milford residents should have more access to that sweet piece of water, so in 1935 he purchased land that had formerly been used as a swimming beach and re-opened it to the public on his own dime.

He built a fishing lodge on Haven Lake, inviting various ice cream moguls to come visit on weekends. He would give them a tour of his factory, showing off his "sincere and honest" local workforce and getting them to sign off deals to buy Bentwood spoons. He called his lodge "The Bentwood Club."

In 1936 the *Wilmington News Journal* reported that Mulholland had been hosting a series of meetings at his lakeside home in an effort to make part or all of Haven Lake a protected refuge for ducks, geese, and other waterfowl. Somewhere along the line here, he took it upon himself to hire a professional to make sure Haven Lake waterfowl were properly fed.

In 1940 the *News Journal* reported on big crowds of people—many of them photographers and film crews—who would stop at Haven Lake to admire its thick flocks of waterfowl. The place was so popular that traffic sometimes came to a standstill along the bridge over the Mispillion River on DuPont Boulevard (now DuPont Highway).

In 1937 Mulholland put his old advertising signage skills to work for Milford. He designed a local variation of the Delaware seal for use as an official city seal. He presented that seal to the City Council as a gift, along with a flag showing the seal. That flag soon went up in the council chambers.

The *Wilmington Morning News*, Sept. 27, 1937: *The old mill ... in the center of the seal is emblematic of the landmark from with this city takes its name. The side characters represent agriculture and navigation. The famous Mispillion oyster crowning the shield, and the clipper ship, represent the early industries of the city.*

That seal is still in use today, as far as I can tell. Mulholland, who died in 1958, was also active with local Freemasons, the Rotary Club, and at Christ Episcopal Church. I believe that one of the Mulholland plant buildings is still standing as of this writing at 2 Marshall Street. It's on the south side of the Mispillion River along Milford's famous Riverwalk, beyond the Vinyard Shipyard site as you are heading toward Goat Island.

Postscript: That Kipling Connection
After witnessing the cow-tending disaster that befell young John Mulholland on his transatlantic voyage in 1887, Rudyard Kipling turned that real-life disaster into a fictional story about a religious conversion, with the lead character ("Mulholland") cutting a deal

with God in exchange for divine intervention.

Mulholland's Contract (1894)

The fear was on the cattle, for the gale was on the sea,
An' the pens broke up on the lower deck an' let the creatures
free—
An' the lights went out on the lower deck, an' no one near but me.

I had been singin' to them to keep 'em quiet there,
For the lower deck is the dangerousest, requirin' constant care,
An' give to me as the strongest man, though used to drink and
swear.

I seed my chance was certain of bein' horned or trod,
For the lower deck was packed with steers thicker'n peas in a
pod,
An' more pens broke at every roll—so I made a Contract with
God.

An' by the terms of the Contract, as I have read the same,
If He got me to port alive I would exalt His Name,
An' praise His Holy Majesty till further orders came.

He saved me from the cattle an' He saved me from the sea,
For they found me 'tween two drownded ones where the roll had
landed me—
An' a four-inch crack on top of my head, as crazy as could be.

But that were done by a stanchion, an' not by a bullock at all,
An' I lay still for seven weeks convalescing of the fall,
An' readin' the shiny Scripture texts in the Seaman's Hospital.

You Wouldn't Believe!

An' I spoke to God of our Contract, an' He says to my prayer:
"I never puts on My ministers no more than they can bear.
"So back you go to the-cattle-boats an' preach My Gospel there.

"For human life is chancy at any kind of trade,
"But most of all, as well you know, when the steers are mad-
afraid;
"So you go back to the cattle-boats an' preach 'em as I've said.

"They must quit drinkin' an' swearin', they mustn't knife on a
blow,
"They must quit gamblin' their wages, and you must preach it so;
"For now those boats are more like Hell than anything else I
know."

I didn't want to do it, for I knew what I should get,
An' I wanted to preach Religion, handsome an' out of the wet,
But the Word of the Lord were laid on me, an' I done what I was
set.

I have been smit an' bruised, as warned would be the case,
An' turned my cheek to the smiter exactly as Scripture says;
But, following that, I knocked him down an' led him up to Grace.

An' we have preaching on Sundays whenever the sea is calm,
An' I use no knife or pistol an' I never take no harm,
For the Lord abideth back of me to guide my fighting arm.

An' I sign for four-pound-ten a month and save the money clear,
An' I am in charge of the lower deck, an' I never lose a steer;

You Wouldn't Believe!

An' I believe in Almighty God an' I preach His Gospel here.

The skippers say I'm crazy, but I can prove 'em wrong,
For I am in charge of the lower deck with all that doth belong—
*Which they would not give to a lunatic, and the competition so
strong!*

THE WILD FLIGHT
OF THE DOVER EIGHT

NOTE: My other books include lots of tales from days gone by. This excerpt from Tubman Travels: 32 Underground Railroad Journeys on Delmarva *details a keystone event from the 1850s, a miraculous escape from the bondage of slavery that was—and still is—celebrated by freedom lovers everywhere.*

The lush expanse of Dover Green has a serene, timeless air about it today. Located at the heart of a celebrated national historic district that is chock full of buildings dating to the 1700s, it has lots of interesting stories to tell about the early days of our country.

Dover was a hotbed of revolutionary activity in those 1700s, as it was here that Delaware earned its nickname, becoming the First State to ratify the Constitution. Those revolutionary tendencies continued into the 1800s arrived, as the state's roads and rivers became key routes along the Underground Railroad. It was here in the 1850s that eight runaway slaves managed a jailbreak that unfolded like something straight out of a Hollywood action movie.

229

The old jail building where all this happened is not standing today, alas. But it was located here at the Green, right next to the Old Statehouse building. Many of the historic buildings nearby were also standing on the night the Dover Eight arrived from Dorchester County, Md. Even the "Green" itself was in place—the open space originated as an outdoor market with vendors, but it had been transformed into a park in 1846.

The story of the Dover Eight's escape from this jail went viral, at least in the 19th century sense of the term. It appeared first in one, then another, and then in countless other newspapers up and down the Atlantic seaboard. Then it spread some more, reaching across the whole country.

Abolitionists up north celebrated the affair with great gusto. Slavery defenders down south were humiliated—and furious. On the Eastern Shore of Maryland, the publicity made a bad year for slave owners even worse. Bad weather in that spring of 1857 had put the growing season at risk. Plus, the Dover Eight affair was no isolated incident—it was just the most famous in a rash of escapes around this time.

At raucous public meetings in Dorchester County and elsewhere, Maryland slave owners demanded that public officials start doing more about "protecting the slave property." They demanded that the police go after anyone and everyone suspected of encouraging or helping runaways.

They also began keeping closer track of the whereabouts of their slaves—and those of their neighbors as well. Without a doubt, some of them decided to dole out a bit of rough and unofficial vigilante justice in the process.

For Harriet Tubman, the dramatic events in Dover were a mixed bag. The work of a conductor had always been dangerous, of course, but the risks of getting captured, jailed, and even killed went up dramatically after the events in Dover.

She was happy for the freedom of so many of her old neighbors in slavery, of course—as we shall see, she may even have provided them with some advice. But she also had more work to do. Her sister Rachel remained in bondage, as did Rachel's children. And then, a little later in the year, Tubman would receive another of those gifts that God was always sending her— this time, a presentiment that her parents might be in danger.

How much risk could she take on in order to bring her family members to freedom? That question grew more difficult after the sensational events in this story.

STORY: The Wild Flight of the Dover Eight

No one knows for sure why Thomas Elliott and Denard Hughes picked the day of March 8, 1857 to make their run from the farm of Pritchett Meredith in Bucktown, Md. Later, Hughes would refer to Meredith as the "hardest man around," so it's easy to speculate about the beatings and whippings they may have endured.

But the decision to run wasn't a rash one made in the heat of a moment—it came only after careful planning. Some historians have speculated that Elliott, Hughes, and the six other Bucktown-area slaves who joined them might have been working with instructions received along the Underground Railroad grapevine from Harriet Tubman herself.

Tubman had spent much of her childhood in Bucktown. The store where she defied an overseer as a young girl and nearly died after getting hit in the head with a two-pound weight was within sight of the Meredith farmhouse. Tubman may well have been acquainted with some members of the Dover Eight, or at least with some of their relatives.

The group set off well-armed with knives and guns. They

most likely stayed on overland routes, probably stopping at the East New Market home of a free black preacher, Samuel Green, and perhaps also at the cabin of Tubman's parents on Poplar Neck, near Preston.

Pritchett Meredith posted a $600 reward for his two slaves. Add in the prizes offered on the other six and the group's capture was worth a cool $3,000. That number proved too tempting for Thomas Otwell, a free black man who had earned Tubman's trust in the past with his work as an Underground Railroad operative. Otwell lived near Milford, in Southern Delaware, where he had recently started renting property from a white man with the last name of Hollis.

The two of them cooked up a scheme to betray the fleeing slaves and walk off with the reward money. Instead of leading the slaves to the next station on their journey to freedom, Otwell took them under cover of night straight into the Dover jail, where he left them in Hollis's hands.

But there was a problem. Otwell had arrived later than expected. The Dover sheriff, a man named Green, was supposed to be on hand when they got there, ready to spring the trap and lock the fugitives behind bars. But Green had given up on Otwell at 2am, heading into his nearby family quarters to get a bit of sleep.

When Otwell arrived at 4 a.m., Hollis tried to coax the slaves into a room where he could lock them up, but one of the fleeing slaves, Henry Predeaux, pointed out in the moonlight of a clear night how the windows in the room were reinforced with iron bars. The runaways stayed in a hallway, growing more suspicious by the minute.

Sheriff Green finally appeared, but he, too, was unable to coax the slaves out of the hallway. He then hurried back to his living quarters in order to retrieve his gun. The slaves followed him right into those living quarters.

There, Predeaux sprang into action, throwing a shovel full of hot coals from the fireplace all over the room and onto a bed. He used a fireplace poker to break out a window, and then he kept the sheriff and Hollis at bay while his compatriots climbed out the window and dropped 12 feet onto the ground outside.

Finally, Predeaux pushed the sheriff away and made a run for the window himself. The sheriff's pistol jammed, and Predeaux, too, made it out of the building. Everyone else was gone by the time his feet hit the ground, so he set out to make his way to Wilmington and the home of famed Underground Railroad conductor Thomas Garrett. That's a journey of 50 miles. Predeaux would soon become the first of the Dover Eight to reach freedom.

Six of the other seven had backtracked, returning along the route that had brought them to Dover. There, they overtook Thomas Otwell and soon were threatening to kill him. Otwell begged for his life. He vowed to get them back on track at the next Underground Railroad stop. Hearing this story later, conductor Thomas Garrett would observe:

It is a wonder that they acted with so much coolness and discretion. One of the men told me he would have killed [Otwell] at once had he not thought, if he did do it, he would have less chance to escape than if they committed no act of violence, which no doubt was a correct view.

The six ended up in the town of Willow Grove, Del. From there, they made their way along forested back roads, eventually reaching the Wilmington area, where Garrett's men managed to find them before the police did. They, too, soon reached freedom in Philadelphia.

That leaves one more. The last of the Dover Eight to find freedom was Lavinia Woolfley. Sometime after making the leap from the jailhouse window, she had become separated from her husband James and the others. She managed to stay in hiding in Delaware for several months before finally finding her way into Pennsylvania. She would eventually be reunited with her husband in Canada.

THE PRESIDENT WHO SHOT DUCKS (AND MARBLES) ON HOG ISLAND

Today, Virginia's barrier islands rank as the longest stretch of undeveloped oceanfront land on the whole East Coast. They are mostly owned by the Nature Conservancy. Visitors can get out there only by boat, of course, and visitation is often restricted to beaches on the outskirts of islands to protect nesting birds raising their young farther inland.

These islands weren't always undeveloped. For centuries, people lived out on Hog, Cobb, and other islands. Most of those folks put food on their tables by fishing, hunting, and gardening, while others worked at coast guard stations, lighthouses, and hunting lodges. Those lodges drew their share of rich and famous visitors.

The President Comes Calling
In November of 1892, Grover Cleveland made history by becoming the first (and still only) candidate to win non-consecutive

presidential elections. He won in 1884, lost in 1888, and then came back to win again.

The president-elect decided to celebrate that last election triumph with a hunting trip to Hog Island. He had been there before with John Sergeant Wise, a prominent lawyer and politician from the opposite side of the political aisle. Here is what Wise had to say about President Cleveland:

I have known him to sit on a calm sunshiny day in a duck blind for ten consecutive hours, with nothing but a simple luncheon to break his fast and nothing but whistlers and buffleheads coming in to his decoys, and return home at night with nothing but a dozen "trash" ducks ... as content and uncomplaining as if he had enjoyed real sport.

On that 1892 trip, the president-elect took the New York, Philadelphia & Norfolk railroad into Exmore, then rode on a carriage over to Willis Wharf, where he boarded a boat to sail to Hog Island. He spent a week and a half out there, engaged in nothing but "recreation and rest."

The *Norfolk Landmark*: *His desire is to be out of reach of office-seekers and cabinet-makers, and no better place for the fulfilling of this desire could be found than this safe retreat."*

The *Norfolk Landmark* again: *Broadwater inlet rang from shore to shore today with the continuous reports of shotgun as Grover Cleveland his fellow sportsmen from the Broadwater club fired at the enormous flocks of wild ducks and brant, [as the waterfowl] wheeled about in surprise and terror."*

Playing for All the Marbles

The trip wasn't perfect. The president-elect sliced his thumb at one point while cocking a gun. A sheriff appeared from the mainland at another point to serve Cleveland with papers from a lawsuit filed against him in a complex breach-of-contract case. There was a stretch in the trip when rain got in the way of Cleveland's various hunting and fishing expeditions.

The people of Hog Island came up with a delectable distraction from that miserable weather. They summoned the best cooks on the island to the president's hunting lodge, where they joined forces to create a "repast [that] has never been excelled," as a reporter for the *New York Herald* put it. The menu included oysters, terrapin, turkey, roast beef, and wildfowl of every variety.

Come dessert time, the islanders served up a true local delicacy, Hog Island figs. Today, there is one variety of fig descended from the trees on the island that is known as the "Grover Cleveland fig" and regarded in foodie circles as quite a delicacy.

That post-election visit was just one of several the president made down to Hog Island over the course of his political career. On another of his visits, the historian Kirk Mariner reports:

[Island resident] Mary Anna Doughty came out of her house to call her four young sons to dinner only to find them shooting marbles in the lane with the President. When she called them in, Cleveland is said to have asked if he too could come, and happily joined the family for a meal of fried pies and milk.

Needless to say, Cleveland was a much-beloved figure on the Lower Eastern Shore. When he won his first election as president, the town of Locustville erected a 65-foot "Cleveland pole." There were big celebratory bonfires in Temperanceville and Mappsville. A cannon was shot off 50 times in Modest Town. In Mearsville, a merchant changed the name of his store to "Cleveland."

That store wasn't the only thing named after the Eastern Shore's favorite president. Several couples named children after him. There was a Grover Cleveland Harris in Exmore, a Grover

You Wouldn't Believe!

Cleveland Tull in Pocomoke City, and a Grover Cleveland Brittingham, also of Pocomoke City.

VARIOUS & SUNDRY!

You Think Getting to the Beach Is a Hassle Nowadays?

Mom, Dad, are we there yet? Was that classic children's whine a thing in the early 1900s? If it was … oh, the poor parents who decided to take their kids on vacation to Bethany Beach, Del.

Everyone complains these days about summertime traffic tie-ups on the way to the beach. But those delays are nothing compared with the trials and tribulations endured by Bethany-bound travelers at the turn of the 20th century.

Life Moved Way Too Fast in 1900

Bethany Beach was brand new back then, and its back story is worth a brief detour. The world was moving so fast as the 1900s began! Think trains, steamboats, and telegraph lines. It was a time, too, when rural folks were moving in droves to big cities. They found themselves living for the first time amid big buildings, noisy factories, and crowded streets. Plus, electricity!

The speed and noise of that "modern" world left lots of

people feeling exhausted, overwhelmed, and depressed. Doctors found a diagnosis for the phenomenon. The theory behind neurasthenia was that human beings weren't meant to live at such a breakneck pace. It was more than our central nervous systems could handle.

Some doctors recommended weeks of bed rest. Others sent patients to sanatorium-like facilities. Another recommendation was rest and relaxation, especially amid the healthy air of the oceanfront.

This is how churches got into the beach-resort business. They were looking to help the faithful navigate the neurasthenic overwhelm in their high-speed lives. Oceanfront destinations already existed, of course, but churches wanted the faithful to head to destinations free from alcohol, frivolity, and sin. An early promotional brochure for Bethany Beach promised:

a haven of rest for quiet people [desiring] wholesome recreation [in a place] without the dissipation found at other more fashionable watering places.

The church resorts were created as oases of renewal. Here, people could reconnect with their true selves, with Mother Nature, and with their savior too. Outside of that Christian angle, the phenomenon wasn't so different from today's boom in meditation and yoga.

Rehoboth Beach was an early example. In the 1870s Rev. Robert Todd of Wilmington, Del. endured a bout of spiritual and physical exhaustion. After a recuperative trip to the New Jersey shore worked wonders for him, Todd returned to the pulpit and announced plans to open a Methodist resort on the Delaware shore.

The Church of Christ got into the act three decades later, when its Christian Missionary Society decided to develop a destination at Bethany Beach. The church bought land, sold lots, and made promises, but the project soon ran into a rough patch. The economy went south in 1901. Banks grew hesitant to loan money. Construction delays popped up. Some of the work that did get done was shoddy.

The Christian Missionary Society was about to bail on the project when some of its members up in Pittsburgh stepped up and took over. They put the project in the hands of some savvy businessmen whom historians would later dub the "Pittsburgh Six." Construction was soon back on track. Wells got dug. A tabernacle went up. A boardwalk opened. Before long, Bethany Beach was scheduling religious-revival events and putting on Chautauqua-like presentations.

The Preacher Tells a Fib
This is when the marketing campaign began in earnest. Here is what Church of Christ bigwig F.D. Power promised would-be travelers in a promotional brochure quoted in the book, *Bethany Beach Memoirs: A Long Look Back:*

There could not be a more picturesque route or a shorter one to the ocean. By B&O to Baltimore: thence by the fine steamer Princess Anne across the Chesapeake for thirty miles ... under the wooded shores of the Isle of Kent to lovely Queenstown, thence for sixty miles by Queen Anne Railroad ... to the ancient city of Lewes and the county of Sussex in Delaware; thence through kaleidoscopic scenery of lovely waters, smiling shores, fertile fields, woods, streams, and lily-starred lakes ...

Bottom line: Preachers can tell whoppers, too. The reality of getting to Bethany Beach was a nightmarish ordeal leavened by fleeting and occasional moments of beauty. In the 1970s, history buffs in Bethany conducted interviews with community elders whose family roots went back to those early Pittsburgh families, including Marjorie Errett and Katherine Willfrey. The stories they tell in the booklet *Bethany Beach, Delaware: A Walk Through History 1901-2014* put to shame any modern-day tales about 10-mile backups at the Chesapeake Bay Bridge or gridlock on Coastal Highway.

First Leg: Train Stations & Poop Walks

Errett's family traveled to the beach during her childhood every June after school let out. They planned to stay through the summer, so the trip involved a gazillion overstuffed suitcases. Clothes, toys, books, linens—everything. Many families brought dogs along.

The Erretts lived a short train ride from Pittsburgh. Marjorie's father would hire someone to cart a single oversized trunk to the local station. Otherwise, every family member, no matter how small, had to lug bags on the walk from home to the station. A 30-minute ride on the rails brought them into Pittsburgh, but the train from there to Baltimore left from a different station.

Everyone grabbed those heavy bags and set off on foot again, this time through city streets. Horses and carriages dominated urban transportation in those days. That looks idyllic in weathered old photos, but those photos are rarely detailed enough to show all the horse poop on the ground. Stepping in a pile or two was inevitable.

Upon arrival in Baltimore after a long train ride through the mountains, day one of the travel endurance test was nearly complete. But first, of course, everyone had to grab those overstuffed suitcases and walk more poop-splotched city streets to a hotel.

Second Leg: Steamboat Bliss

The next morning started like the movie *Groundhog Day*, with everyone schlepping bags through poop-splotched city streets. At the steamboat terminal in Baltimore's Inner Harbor, the Erretts would often meet up with church friends who'd come in by train from the Washington, D.C. area.

If the weather was good, the three-hour ride across the Chesapeake Bay was a blissful respite amid this ordeal. The scenery was awe-inspiring. Creature comforts abounded. Another bonus awaited at Love Point on Kent Island. There, the railroad line ran right next to the steamship landing, so the carting of bags was minimal. If, however, the weather was not so good ... well, think seasick children.

Third Leg: Black Cinders and Ashes

You might think the railroad trip across the Delmarva countryside would offer another blissful interlude, but no such luck. This was the age of steam-powered locomotives—and this was summertime. There was no air conditioning. The windows were all open.

The engine up front belched up huge billows of smoke and soot. One railroad line across the Eastern Shore at this time was called the Baltimore, Chesapeake, and Atlantic—or BCA. Passengers used to joke that the acronym stood for something else—Black Cinders and Ashes.

Families bound for Bethany inhaled that smoke the whole way. Getting off of the train in Rehoboth Beach, they had to beat their own clothing like a rug, sending puffs of dust and ashes up into the air.

Fourth Leg: Waiting and Puttering

Today, the run from Rehoboth Beach to Bethany Beach is a proverbial hop, skip, and jump in the car. But there was no roadway bridge across Indian River Bay in the early 1900s. No railroad line extended across the water, either. (This latter improvement was something the Church of Christ and the Pittsburgh Six powers worked on like crazy, but they were unable to convince a railroad company to get on board.)

And so upon arriving at the train platform in downtown Rehoboth, everyone had to ... sit back and do nothing. According to Ms. Errett, they were instructed to wait for the arrival of another train from Philadelphia so that more Bethany travelers could join in this next leg of the journey.

Only then did everyone climb up into a "big horse-drawn bus" that then waddled its way up Rehoboth Avenue to a man-made waterway, the Lewes Rehoboth Canal. There they boarded a mini-steamship called the *Atlantic* (later, another vessel called the *Allie May* came on the scene). These little steamers puttered along the Canal, then through Rehoboth Bay and Indian River Bay before finally winding up White's Creek to a place called Pennewell's Landing. If the weather cooperated those travelers who could stay awake enjoyed some spectacular scenery. If the weather didn't cooperate, well ... think seasick children.

Fifth Leg: Bugging Out
The mini-steamer left travelers two miles from Bethany Beach. They climbed up into another horse-drawn bus. This last leg of the journey was mostly atop sand and marshland, so it took two excruciating hours. Along the way came endless bone-jarring bumps and thumps that had a way of aggravating the seasickness felt by children fresh from a boat ride. Throughout, sand flies and mosquitoes swarmed over the travelers.

Then, at long last: Welcome to Bethany Beach!

In what seems to me like a bit of understatement, Ms. Errett described the two-day trip as "completely exhausting." Everyone went straight to bed upon arrival. There, they drifted off to sleep amid memories of "smoky and dusty trains, squall-tossed boat rides through narrow waterways, wagons lurching through sand and dust, plagues of sand flies and mosquitoes, and"—you guessed it—"seasick children."

The End of the Ordeal
The easing of the Bethany Beach travel nightmare happened slowly but surely as the decades went on. In 1910, a new Bethany Beach Loop Canal allowed travelers to bypass that last excruciating horse-drawn bus ride. Instead, the Allie May would drop travelers right in the middle of town. In the 1920s, the newly constructed Route 26 (Atlantic Avenue/Garfield Parkway) offered an alternative route to automobile travelers. The first bridge over the Indian River Inlet opened in 1934.

Perhaps I should close by returning to that Church of Christ preacher and his whopper of a travel description full of "smiling shores and lily-starred lakes." Well, at the end of that wildly inaccurate bit of advertising, Rev. Power did make it back into the light of truth. This is his description of the trip's final destination:

... and then the great ocean, with its splendid beach, its surf, its varied scenery, its manifold voices, its majesty, and its healing and refreshment.

Amen, reverend.

FLYING MAYONNAISE JARS!

I frequently go on the WBOC-TV show *Delmarva Life* to tell stories of days gone by on "Throwback Thursdays." Hosts Jimmy Hoppa and Lisa Bryant gave me a homework assignment in advance of one segment during a week when UFO sightings were all over the news: Did flying saucers and little green men have a history on the Delmarva Peninsula?

That's my kind of homework!

The Blue Light Special

Back in 1860, the sky was still just the sky. No airplanes or helicopters soared overhead. Folks might have heard about hot air balloons, but they were still a newfangled European thing, more rumor than reality on our shores.

Imagine, then, how disorienting it must have been on the hot summer night of July 13 when a pale blue light appeared, streaking across the Upper Delaware sky.

According to the *Wilmington Tribune*, this blue light special moved steadily from northwest to southeast at an altitude of 100 feet. Behind it was a trio of "very red and glowing balls." That turned into a quartet when the back end of this blue light pooped out a fourth red ball, which then fell into a seemingly organized formation with the other balls.

The incident lasted a full minute, with the phenomenon moving over the Delaware River and, eventually, out of sight.

This was the earliest Delmarva UFO sighting that I came across. There were dozens and dozens of other sightings reported in old newspapers through the decades that followed. The 1940s were flying-saucer-sighting boom times. Orson Welles had done his infamous *War of the Worlds* radio broadcast in 1938. The atomic bombs of the 1940s probably pushed folks into a science-fiction frame of mind as well.

But most of those reports are, well, boring. Someone somewhere saw an object in the sky that looked like a dinner plate or, indeed, a saucer. Sometimes, the flying mystery had a little exhaust tail. Usually, they moved at dizzying speeds. It's the same old story over and over again.

The Jar Head from Rehoboth

One report stands out, however. On another hot summer night—July 8, 1947—Forrest Wenyon, a pilot from Rehoboth Beach, reported a UFO sighting that didn't fit the drab pattern. He was flying his plane at 1,000 feet when a cylinder-shaped monstrosity zipped by.

Asked by the *Wilmington Morning News* to describe the object, Wenyon chose an unlikely analogy. This was a "flying mayonnaise jar," he said, complete with what looked like a twist-on lid. The jar flew in bottom-first fashion, leaving behind a trail of silver flames.

The tail appeared to be a lid which had been perforated and ... from these perforations the flames escaped. In a matter of two, at the most three, seconds the object had disappeared over and past Fort Miles.

Wenyon had a bit of conspiracy theorist about him. He had read in the papers recently about a tragic plane crash on the Western Shore of Maryland.

He studied the stories of that accident carefully and believes now that the tail disintegration in mid-air [of that doomed airplane], reported by a number of witnesses, was the result of a "direct hit" by a "jar."

Like so many other UFO enthusiasts through the years, Wenyon worried that these flying mayonnaise jars might be part of some top-secret government experiment gone awry. Those fears grew more intense as people in government offices failed to heed his dire warnings.

Mr. Wenyon ... called the Federal Bureau of Investigation [to tell them about the flying mayonnaise jars]. They were not interested, and told him so. He then called ... the Civil Aeronautic Authority, ... which gave him a sympathetic hearing, thanked him, and said they'd investigate. To date he has received no answer.

I mean, what other than a vast secret conspiracy could possibly explain their lack of interest in pursuing the possibility of an imminent mayonnaise-jar catastrophe?

Postscript: Welles's 'War'

The panic sparked by that Orson Welles radio broadcast of the *War of the Worlds* on Oct. 30, 1938 is not an urban legend. The next day, the *Wilmington (Del.) Morning News* reported on moments of panic that unfolded all around the city. One man rushed into a "mid-city restaurant and created a near panic by excitedly announcing the invasion from Mars" and warning, "They'll be here any minute!" Another man broke into a church service rescue, snatching up his mother and vowing to "take her to safety.'"

You Wouldn't Believe!

In *True Tales of the Eastern Shore*, historian Kirk Mariner describes a scene in a corner store in Accomac, Va. A crowd of regulars gathered there every Sunday to spread gossip, tell tales, and listen to the radio. When the store owner walked into this scene in the middle of Welles' broadcast, he saw a sea of "ashen" faces, including that of the county sheriff.

Upon digesting the bad news that Martian invaders had landed, the store owner then ran upstairs to get his gun. While there, his wife used these words to try to calm him down:

Invaded by whom? Those little men? We'll handle them!

REFUGE OF SCOUNDRELS: REEDY ISLAND

The streets of Port Penn, Del. present pleasing, peaceful scenes at every turn: views of the broad Delaware River, adorable old houses, yards dotted with boats and watermen gear. It's easy to imagine during a stroll that you've passed through a time portal into an 1800s fishing village.

But be careful during your time travels! Just off the shore here is a spit of land called Reedy Island, and that place has a long history of serving as a hideout for unsavory visitors. Think ruthless pirates, enemy sailors, despicable critters, and infectious diseases.

A Den of Pirates

The Delaware Bay and River served as a commercial superhighway in colonial times. Philadelphia ranked back then among the most populous and prosperous cities on the Eastern seaboard, and the cargo aboard merchant ships bound for that city proved an irresistible target for piracy. Among the privateers who came calling on Delaware were a couple whose names live on in pirate lore today—Captain Kidd and Blackbeard.

But the pirate who probably struck the most terror into the local population was the lesser-known Don Vincent Lopez. This Spaniard's reign of terror began in May of 1748 when he showed up at the mouth of the Delaware Bay with a handful of ships. The main brig in that fleet, *Saint Michael*, had 14 guns. His crew numbered 160, a mix of Spaniards, Englishmen, Irishmen, and black men.

Don Vincent's timing was impeccable. The British man-of-war assigned to protect all the valuable cargo headed to and from Philadelphia was undergoing repairs. Finding himself free to do what pirates do, Don Vincent captured one sloop called *Three Brothers*. That didn't go so well, actually. The men he left in charge of the prize got drop-dead drunk, allowing the imprisoned captain to retake his ship and sail into Lewes.

Undeterred, Don Vincent captured several other sloops and schooners. In his *History of Delaware*, John Thomas Sharf writes:

The long list of outrages of this character was daily increased by reports of [new] outrages [even] more daring and impudent.

Then Don Vincent made a move that previous pirates hadn't dared to do—he sailed brazenly all the way up the bay and into the Delaware River. He had his eye on the town of New Castle and the merchant ships docked there. As he approached town, one of the prisoners he had on board, George Proctor, jumped overboard and swam to shore. A couple of historians speculate that this was actually part of Don Vincent's plan, that he wanted an escapee to go out and spread panic and fear among the population. That's exactly what happened. Writing in the *Wilmington Morning News* in 1967, W. Emerson Wilson says that

Proctor regaled the people of New Castle with "lurid tales about how the pirate would burn the town and massacre the inhabitants if they dared to resist."

But the people of New Castle did not go weak at the knees. When Don Vincent sailed into range, four cannons opened fire. From Sharf's *History of Delaware*:

Lopez, finding that his reception would be rather warm if he ventured nearer, slipped his cables and dropped down the river.

The dastardly Don Vincent found refuge on ... Reedy Island.

Operating from that new base, his pirates soon boarded four ships. In one case, the "pirates stripped the ship and the crew, taking every bit of clothing they had" and then "put all the naked men ashore." Don Vincent ventured over to the New Jersey side, too, putting men in longboats so that they could travel inland along smaller rivers to raid homes and towns. W. Emerson Wilson again:

[Don Vincent] was so successful in all of his ventures that some of his English prisoners were persuaded to join him, ... trying their hand at a little piracy.

Traffic through the bay and river came to a standstill. As word spread of Don Vincent's depredations, the British finally sent two Royal Navy men-of-war down from New England. Don Vincent exchanged fire with those warships, but soon realized that he didn't stand a chance. Most of his fleet was captured or sunk, but Don Vincent himself managed to escape.

Ironically, he is in part responsible for ending the age of piracy in Delaware. Multiple British warships remained at the mouth of the bay in the wake of Don Vincent's months-long reign of terror. Those ships beat back every pirate ship dumb enough to show its sails. Delaware's newspapers contain sporadic reports about minor bits of piracy into the 1780s after which the reports peter out altogether. Don Vincent was the last of the villains to cause a real ruckus.

Warship on the Run

Boston and Philadelphia always get star billing in histories of the early days of the American Revolution, but the Delmarva Peninsula played a brief (and triumphant) little role in 1776. By that point the British had assigned two warships to patrol the mouth of the Delaware Bay, but they weren't hunting pirates this time. Their mission was to keep ammunition and supplies from getting up to Philadelphia.

The blockade was leaky. Lots of boats snuck through under cover of fog and darkness, especially smaller vessels captained by experienced locals who knew how to keep to waters that were too shallow for big warships.

The British commander, Captain Andrew Hammond, soon had another problem on his hands. His ships, *Roebuck* and *Liverpool*, were running short of freshwater. By most accounts, that's why, on the morning of May 8, Hammond started sailing up the Delaware Bay. Another school of thought says that, yes, Hammond needed water, but he also had his eye on a military prize— the powder mill operated by the DuPont family up in Wilmington.

Hearing of Hammond's movements, the Pennsylvania Committee of Safety went into all-hands-on-deck mode, ordering "every Boat & Soldier to their stations, and each to prepare for immediate action." The Brits got up to Wilmington without incident. They anchored near "Christiana Creek," or the Christina River to us. There, as a morning fog lifted, Captain Hammond spied a fleet of 15 ships headed his way. But he wasn't worried:

The vessels were "all tiny." They appeared "neither formidable nor impressive."

But the Americans were peskier than Hammond anticipated. Their little boats stuck mostly to shallow water. Sprinting in for occasional attacks, they presented challenging targets, tiny and fast-moving. Meanwhile, the Americans did pretty well in firing at the big, slow-moving warships. Things took a terrible turn for Captain Hammond as he ran aground while trying to maneuver *Roebuck* out of trouble. The Americans might have moved in for the kill if they weren't short of ammunition.

The battle had lasted four hours. Giddy spectators on the shore cheered every American move during the action. A Philadelphia newspaper crowed:

The greatest praises were given to the courage and spirit of our officers and men by the many thousand spectators who lined the shore on both sides of the river.

Hammond expected that fight to continue the next morning, when he was greeted with the sight of American boats arrayed across the river in battle formation. Now back afloat thanks to a high tide, Hammond headed south, hoping to draw his enemies into deeper waters. The Americans didn't take the bait.

The Brits found refuge at … Reedy Island.

There, they surveyed the damage. One of their sailors was dead. Six were wounded. Both ships suffered serious damage. An American prisoner on *Roebuck*, William Barry, later reported that "many shots [landed] betwixt the wind and water: some went quite through [the ship], some in her quarter, and [she] was much raked fore and aft."

A Philadelphia newspaper reported that "our cannon did great execution to their hulls," and "they were obliged to keep their carpenters patching and mending for two days after."

The Brits did some damage out of their new Reedy Island HQ, capturing and destroying some small vessels. But they'd lost the larger battle. The patriot and future president John Adams wrote to his wife, Abigail:

There has been a gallant Battle, in Delaware River between the Gallies and two Men of War, the Roebuck *and* Liverpool, *in which the Men of War came off second best—which has diminished, in the Minds of the People, on both sides of the River, the Terror of a Man of War.*

Alas, the joy that erupted on Delaware Bay over this battle would soon give way to gloom. Before the year was out, General George Washington's Continental Army would suffer a disastrous defeat at New York, followed by an ignominious retreat. The Americans would get another chance to gloat in the end, but not until passing through a long stretch of dark and desperate times.

Nothing to Crow About

Most of us modern-day folks don't really care about crows one way or the other, but those birds ranked as a public enemy in past centuries. This was especially true among farmers—hence, the scarecrow. Government-sanctioned crow hatred dates at least as far back as the 1500s, when the powers that be in England adopted a Preservation of Grain Act to protect farm harvests. That law would evolve into a requirement that every man, woman, and child in the country kill the animals on a list of crop-destroying "vermin."

Crows landed high on that list. Towns that failed to hit their annual dead-crow quota were punished with fines levied on city coffers. Crow hatred came to our shores with the colonists. During the 18th and 19th centuries, Delaware, Maryland, and Virginia all paid generous bounties to hunters for crow carcasses.

Virginia even accepted crow scalps as payment in lieu of taxes.

Every fall a slew of crows from various points north migrated to the Chesapeake and Delaware bays. In an 1886 article in *American Naturalist*, a New Jersey bird lover named Samuel Rhoads described the tendency of most of those crows to form winter roosts amid the dense forests of places like the New Jersey Pine Barrens. But Rhoads also takes note of an odd minority. One "murder" of crows—that really is the correct name for a gaggle of the birds—preferred to roost on a low-lying island in the Delaware River.

The earliest report of that winter roost came from the "father of American ornithology," Alexander Wilson, in the 1790s. He placed the population at that time on Pea Patch Island, a little north of Port Penn and Reedy Island:

[This] low, flat, alluvial spot of a few acres [is] elevated but little above high-water mark and covered with a thick growth of reeds. This appears to be the grand rendezvous or headquarters of the greater part of the crows within forty or fifty miles of the spot. It is entirely destitute of trees, the crows alighting and nestling among the reeds, which by these means are broken down and matted together.

Wilson also reported on a catastrophe that had struck that roost "some years" before when a furious nor'easter storm flooded the island. Rather than fleeing that night, the crows opted to hold for dear life onto those thin, matted reeds of marsh grasses. It did not go well.

Thousands of them were seen the next day floating in the river. ... For miles, they blackened the whole [New Jersey] shore.

The oddball crows stuck with their marshy habits in spite of the disaster. As soon as their population rebounded, they were flocking to Pea Patch Island in "as immense multitudes as ever."

You Wouldn't Believe!

What finally drove the birds from Pea Patch was the one-two punch of hunting and development. In the early 1800s, a local newspaper reported that a man named John Deputy promised local officials that he would "kill or banish" all crows from the island for a fee of $500. I have seen no report on whether he succeeded, but the crows' days on Pea Patch Island ended for sure in 1814, when construction began on the military outpost that would become Fort Delaware.

The banished crows found refuge ... on Reedy Island.

In his mid-1830s *Manual of the Ornithology of the United States and Canada*, another famed naturalist, Thomas Nuttall, reported watching the black birds arrive on Reedy in "vast numbers." George W. Jones, a lighthouse keeper on Reedy Island, reported that this "murder" was so dense that birds blanketed 20 of the island's 65 acres, "breaking down the reeds, which are from seven to nine feet tall, and roosting upon the broken stems."

My last note on these scoundrels is a matter of justice. The crows were innocent of the charges lodged against them. The 1899 *Yearbook of the Department of Agriculture* reported on a scientific study of the contents of 1,000 crow stomachs. Those scientists did find some corn, fruit, and poultry eggs. But more than 90 percent of the corn was waste corn from the ground, not the good stuff bound for human tables. The amount of fruit and eggs was "trivial." Conclusion:

On the other hand, many noxious insects and mice were eaten. The verdict was therefore rendered in favor of the crow, since, on the whole, the bird seemed to do more good than harm.

But by the time that report came out, the birds had been driven from their beloved Reedy refuge. Here, too, they were done in by a development project—in 1886, the federal government started construction on a massive quarantine station on

Reedy Island, the topic we will come to in three, two, one …

Infectious!

Reedy Island provided a different kind of refuge once that quarantine station got up and running. The 1880s and 1890s saw immigrants coming to America in unprecedented numbers, to the tune of nearly 10 million new arrivals, mostly from Europe—triple the rate of the 1870s. The surge of newcomers kept up until the 1920s.

This influx of immigrants began arriving just as the fields of medicine and public health were taking their modern forms. Scientists had begun to get a handle on the workings of bacteria and infectious diseases. No longer did they blame epidemics on miasma, or "bad air." This revelation came at a time when the federal government was growing by leaps and bounds, taking on new responsibilities and enacting ambitious new programs. It was boom times for public health initiatives, many of which were aimed at preventing diseases from coming ashore with those newly arrived immigrants.

Once that federal quarantine station opened on Reedy Island in 1893, every international vessel headed up the Delaware River had to stop there for inspection. The boats docked beside a 200-foot-long pier. A large shed on that pier was full of disinfecting chemicals and gear. A boiler provided steam power to hoses filled with water and gases.

A little hospital stood out there, too, along with offices and housing for workers. The buildings were all elevated on stilts and connected by bridge-like gangways. A telegraph line ran to Port Penn, the nearest mainland town, delivering updates about potentially dangerous pathogens.

The primary targets here were the stuff of deadly epidemics—think cholera, tuberculosis, bubonic plague, and smallpox. In 1919, the *Wilmington Morning Star* newspaper described the work that went into killing disease-carrying rodents:

Particular attention was paid to prevent the spread of plagues, especially the bubonic plague. In order to prevent ... this plague, gases were formed in holds of all incoming vessels so that any rats that might be in the hold would be killed. The rats are the worst carriers of the plague and after each ship would receive the gassing, hundreds of rats would be found dead in various parts of the hold.

The gas involved here was sulfur dioxide. One of the quarantine station's vessels was reserved for transporting those carcasses, though the paper gave no indication of the location of the rodent killing fields where those bodies were dumped.

The staffers on Reedy Island probably operated on a smaller scale in the manner of Ellis Island, which is where my grandparents ran the medical-inspection gauntlet described by Howard Markel and Alexandra Minna Stern in a 2002 edition of a health policy journal, *The Milbank Quarterly.*

Physicians monitored the steady stream of immigrants filing through the labyrinth of fenced-in areas, on the lookout for a list of medical and psychiatric conditions... For example, one physician was stationed near an entryway, accessible only by stairs, where he could scrutinize newcomers hauling their suit-cases and possessions for signs of shortness of breath and cardiac problems. Another physician carefully inspected the neck size and shape of those queuing before him for evidence of goiter. Yet another examined newcomers for rashes on the skin, nails, and scalp that might indicate ringworm, favus, and other fungal infec-tions.

Most vividly recalled by immigrants, however, was the

dreaded eye examination for trachoma, which involved evert-
ing the eyelid with either the physician's fingers or an implement
akin to a buttonhook. Commonly used instruments were stetho-
scopes and, after 1910, x-rays, which aided in the identification
of pulmonary tuberculosis. Similarly, the tools of the bacteriol-
ogy laboratory, such as microscopes, slides, stains, and culture
methods, were regularly used at American immigration centers
during the first two decades of the 20th century. These apparatus
were crucial to the diagnosis of sexually transmitted diseases, like
gonorrhea and syphilis, and parasitic infections, like hookworm.
[U.S. Public Health Service] physicians also looked for insanity,
hernias, rheumatism, senility, malignancies, varicose veins, poor
eyesight or blindness, and a range of other infirmities.

Things slowed down on the immigration front in the
1920s, when the federal government adopted new and much
stricter caps on newcomers. Those limits remained in place
through the Depression and World War II.

The quarantine station on Reedy Island closed in the
1950s. Several buildings were eventually moved onto the mainland in Port Penn and turned into private homes. If you want to
see them, the Commodore's House is at 4 N. Congress St., while
a barracks house for unmarried workers and an officer's house are
next to each other at 111 and 113 S. Congress St.

As far as I know, Reedy Island has not housed any pirates, enemy
ships, giant crow roosts, or infectious diseases in more recent
decades.

THE YEAR SMALLPOX RUINED CHRISTMAS

The people of Sussex County, Delaware did not have a very merry Christmas in 1919. Their holidays that year were instead filled with fear, distrust, and contention, culminating in a near-riot in mid-January of 1920 on the historic town circle of Georgetown, the county seat.

The story begins in early December when reports surfaced that a contagious infection had popped up near Millsboro. At first, everyone thought it was probably chickenpox. At worst, perhaps it was the "Cuban itch," a milder cousin of the smallpox virus known by scientists as alastrim.

No such luck: State health officials soon confirmed 20 cases of smallpox. There were no fatalities in the early days of the outbreak, but public health experts knew better than to underestimate a disease that ranks as the deadliest in human history.

First Steps: Quarantines and Roadblocks
The outbreak was located in a geographic area known by its odd-sounding name from colonial times, the "Indian River Hundred."

One newspaper account put ground zero amid the "colonies of Moors" living in the countryside outside Millsboro. (In its most precise sense, that word Moors refers to very specific communities populated by folks with significant Native American ancestry. Sometimes, however, it has been used more loosely, as a catch-all term that might encompass African Americans and Mexican Americans as well.)

Once smallpox was confirmed, the public-health hammer started coming down just as local families were gearing up for the coming holiday season.

• Households with confirmed cases of smallpox were quarantined for weeks on end, with no one allowed in or out.

• The town of Millsboro stationed police officers along roads to try and prevent the arrival of people from smallpox-infested areas.

• The state banned all shipments of holiday wreaths and greens, which really hurt families in Sussex County—those greens were a big seasonal side business at that time, helping to pay for gifts and holiday meals.

• There was also talk of more drastic measures on the horizon, such as keeping all trains from stopping at certain stations or issuing quarantine orders that extended beyond disease-ridden households to encompass whole neighborhoods or even entire towns.

Newspaper reports on Dec. 8 had the situation improving. No new cases had been diagnosed beyond the 20 in the initial report. The authorities even started allowing a few shipments of holiday wreaths out of the area, though not before the greens had been thoroughly fumigated.

Mob Rule in Georgetown

Alas, the good-news respite was short-lived. By Dec. 11 alarm bells were ringing more loudly than ever: "Every person in the [Indian River] Hundred is going to be vaccinated or be arrested," announced state health commissioner Chester H. Wells. In Millsboro, everyone was required to carry a certificate of vaccination while in public places.

The timing of the next big development here is not exactly clear in the newspaper accounts I've reviewed, but somewhere in the weeks that followed health inspectors came to the conclusion that there was a lot more smallpox around than first thought—a couple of hundred cases, in fact. In response, they decided to create a "belt of safety" around the disease.

On Dec. 19, the state ordered vaccinations for every single person in the five "hundreds" surrounding Indian River—those hundreds were Lewes and Rehoboth, Broadkill, Georgetown, Dagsboro, and Baltimore. The "belt of safety" was a big one then, stretching from down in Selbyville to up in Milton and over to Georgetown. Folks within the belt were given until Dec. 27 to get to their doctors and get vaccinated—or risk getting arrested.

Merry Christmas, one and all!

Newspaper guesstimates at the time put compliance with the order at about 75 percent of the population. The situation blew up on Jan. 14, 1920. Health Commissioner Wells came down to Georgetown from Dover that day to supervise the ongoing enforcement of the vaccination order, but he found that things were going much more slowly than he wanted. He visited 40 shops along Main Street and found at least 10 workers there who could not produce vaccination papers.

In an ominous development, Wells was unable to find a single police officer or any other town official who would help him serve arrest warrants on the slackers. That evening, at 7pm, the health commissioner was reading a newspaper in the Brick Hotel on the Circle when hundreds of angry residents descended on the downtown. Soon, the hotel lobby was packed with angry Sussex men and women. Scores of others remained outside, screaming things like "run him out" and "get a rope" and "we won't be vaccinated."

Inside, a man wearing a military uniform confronted Wells:

Will you go peaceably? For if you don't we'll put you out of town by force.

Wells gathered up his coat and papers, convinced that "if I resisted there would have been a riot." Several men escorted him to a car and drove him to Milford. That vehicle, Wells said, was so well "covered with mud" that "I could not even learn the license number."

Wait, What Just Happened?

Lots of conflicting reports arose later about what happened that night. Was it really 300 people? Did the mob really include many "of the town's leading citizens"? Perhaps Commissioner Wells, as the mayor of Georgetown contended, got "cold feet" and showed a lack of "nerve"?

Another question: Were the men who escorted Wells to a car really on the wrong side of the law? One newspaper summed up the other side of the story in rather comical fashion:

It was not a mob. It was just a friendly little party of Dr. Wells' friends who called to pay their respects and give him a head's up that a few 'evil-minded folks' might do him bodily injury.

There was some public fallout in the aftermath. The top

265

aide to the state's attorney general resigned amid insinuations that, as a Georgetown native, he had been overly sympathetic to the recalcitrant locals. Similarly, the entire local health board in Georgetown resigned en masse in late January, with the same suspicions circling around their departures.

A new local health board was soon installed. While I saw nothing in my reading that came right out and said explicitly that state and local officials had reached a backroom compromise to end the dispute, that's what it looks like to my eyes. State officials got to claim some scalps by way of those resignations, while that new local health board got to keep the local peace by announcing that considering the fact there were no cases of the disease in Georgetown, no one would be arrested going forward for not being vaccinated.

By the end of February, just two cases of smallpox remained in Delaware—and both were well quarantined. The crisis had passed.

Postscript: Georgetown and Anti-Vaxxers

I am feeling a need to add a detailed footnote here. In my searching for information about this incident, I came across several brief references to it in history articles tracing the background of the often-reviled "anti-vaccination" movement of our modern days. Here is one example of how the events in Georgetown in 1919 get handled in those histories:

Around the same time, it became apparent that not everyone was comfortable with the practice of vaccination. Whilst, as today, most people saw most vaccines as exceptional success stories there were those who resisted vaccination, especially compulsory vaccination. In one example of energetic opposition to mandatory inoculation in the US, an armed mob led by a retired army lieutenant ran health officers out of Georgetown, Delaware.

This strikes me as quite unfair, based on my review of twenty or so contemporary accounts of that smallpox Christmas season in Sussex County. A lot of local folks did take exception to the vaccination order, but the situation doesn't read to me like that opposition came from some bunch of conspiracy-minded numbskulls. If I could play defense attorney, here are a few points I would make:

• Many residents remained convinced that the disease at hand was chickenpox, not smallpox. A group of private citizens, in fact, brought in their own outside expert to try and prove those suspicions true.

• Whether by accident or incompetence, the state health officials who put the outbreak at 20 cases in the early days had seriously underestimated the problem. As it turned out, there were 10 times that many cases. A mistake like right out of the gate doesn't exactly generate lasting trust among the public.

• While the smallpox vaccine in various forms had been around for more than a century, the treatment still had a dicey reputation at this point in its development—and for good reason. It failed to protect the health of some people, due to improper storage and preparation of doses. When improperly prepared, it sometimes transmitted other infections, including tetanus, syphilis, and tuberculosis. These problems with the vaccine wouldn't be solved until later in the 20th century.

• If you were living in a place like Georgetown on the outskirts of the "safety belt," where no one had seen any cases of smallpox anywhere near their town, such risks might have loomed larger in your mind than they would have if you lived in disease-ridden Millsboro.

• To make matters worse, it seems that some state health

officials acted like jerks, refusing to cut anyone any slack, no matter how genuine the complications in life that led them to delay vaccination.

• Those same state health officials apparently never told anyone that by law, the state of Delaware was supposed to pay medical bills associated with the vaccination order. This revelation seems to have spread through town like wildfire in the run-up to the "riot," with lots of talk in the air about how poor families had to skimp on Christmas to pay for vaccinations that by law were supposed to be provided by the state.

• Here in our modern times, we have grown accustomed to things like required school-age vaccinations, but a century ago many civil-libertarian types regarded such orders as an overly authoritarian intrusion into the private sphere of a family's medical decisions, especially given the very real risks associated with the much-less-than-perfect vaccine concoctions that were in use back then. In both Europe and a number of states in this country, the earliest laws requiring certain vaccinations were almost immediately repealed in the face of vociferous protests that came from across the political spectrum, left and right alike.

OK, the defense rests. The larger story of smallpox has a happy ending of course. Long an endemic disease in almost every part of the world, smallpox killed an estimated 300 million people in the 20th century alone. Imperfect though they were, the early vaccines made a dent and helped put the disease on its heels. Safer and more effective vaccine strategies in place by the mid-20th century killed the killer off altogether. By 1980 the disease had been eradicated from every corner of the world.

INVASION OF THE WHEELMEN, 1896

The endurance army descends on my town of Cambridge, Md. twice a year, once for the Eagleman triathlon in the summer and then again for the Ironman Maryland extravaganza in the fall. Everywhere you turn during those weekends, multi-thousand-dollar bikes are hanging off of cars and trucks. Hotels are booked solid. Restaurants are dishing out carb-heavy meals.

Cycling events are the rage these days, from Le Tour de Shore down in Virginia to the Bay to Bay Bike Ride on Maryland's Upper Eastern Shore. When this trend started taking off in the early 2000s, it felt to me like a new, modern phenomenon. But that was before I learned about the great "Wheelman" convention of 1896.

'A Continual Round of Pleasures'

Put on by a group called the Maryland Division Wheelmen, that combination convention and racing event likely holds the honor of being the biggest sporting event in the history of Cambridge. Depending on which account you read, between 5,000 and 10,000 riders rolled into "Groove City" for the 4th of July holiday that year.

The affair unfolded in the midst of a nationwide craze over bicycling and received front-page coverage over the course of several days in the big-city *Baltimore Sun:*

The wheelmen and citizens of hospitable and beautiful Cambridge have made this first day of the Maryland Division meet of 1896 a continual round of pleasures as varied as delightful. Since the early morning everybody has been extremely busy having a good time.

Bicyclists came from the western shore aboard a run of steamboat trips scheduled especially for the occasion. Two boats left Baltimore on July 2, four left Baltimore on July 3, and two more left in the early morning hours of July 4. At least one other boat came from St. Mary's, Md. lower down on the western shore. Riders also arrived from points north via a slew of extra trains that rolled in from Seaford, Del.

At 6 a.m., the ... steamer Tivoli arrived with 500 cyclists and their friends on board. A delightfully cool breeze was blowing off the water as the excursionists came ashore, and leaping upon their wheels they came gliding swiftly up the smooth, shady High street to their hotels or boarding places.

At a welcome reception in town on the courthouse green, the host town's official "greeter," Alonzo L. Miles, told riders:

The freedom of the city is yours. Our homes are open to you and our hearts will respond to your every reasonable desire while you are with us.

Chinese Lanterns, Waterfront Dances, and a 'Grand Parade'
The two official days of the meet included competitive racing, casual rides, and lots of parties. On the afternoon of July 3, the

president of Baltimore's Continental Bank, Wilbur Jackson, invited the cyclists to ride 10 miles or so out in the countryside to visit his waterfront summer home at Castle Haven, where he had a Baltimore caterer serve lunch on "large tables under the shady trees on the lawn."

Here is a newspaper description of the grand ball that began at 10 p.m. on July 3:

At the end of Long Wharf, an island almost fully one-eighth of a mile out in the Choptank, connected only with the mainland by a narrow causeway, the new dancing pavilion is lighted with many colored lights and presents a beautiful picture from the main. It seems an enchanted palace resting upon the placid water of the river whose brilliant lights are reflected in myriad sparkles in the water. [Clarification: The reference to "Long Wharf" here is likely a mistake—to the best of my knowledge, the only pavilion set out in the water at that time was a little way northwest of Long Wharf, at the Oakley Beach Hotel. The hotel burned down in the 1950s.]

The whole town was decked out in gloriously welcoming fashion for the Wheelmen. In addition to everpresent swaths of red, white, and blue and the state colors of orange and black, there were:

Chinese lanterns by the thousands swinging in the breeze from the broad verandas, the eaves of the houses, in the trees, and everywhere.

On July 4 the wheelmen made a meandering "grand parade" through town along a dozen different streets. In addition to standard bikes, there were tandem, triplet, and quadruplet contraptions on display. The parade ended on the waterfront, where 100 bushels of oysters and 10 barrels of crabs were waiting.

The competitions on Wheelman weekend included sprint

races in addition to the long-distance affairs that are popular nowadays. A short, one-third-of-a-mile-long racing track—the "only one in the state of the latest type"—was surrounded by bleachers seating more than 3,000 fans.

The most exciting race of the meet was a two-mile division championship in which two of the top contenders hailed from Cambridge.

The rivalry between the two Cambridge men is so great that the town is practically divided into rooters for one or the other. When the race ended, their friends, eager to learn the decision, jumped over the stands and swarmed up on the track. When Phelps was declared the winner, pandemonium broke loose. Elderly men threw their hats in the air, others turned somersaults, and cheer after cheer was given.

Postscript: The Clifton Wheelmen Go To Jail

Every spare space in town was used to accommodate guests. One hotel even "obtained the use of two large school buildings, which have been filled with cots." Still, not everyone had a perfect trip: A group from Baltimore called the "Clifton Wheelmen"—presumably a reference to the neighborhood of that name—thought they had hotel rooms secured in advance, but found out otherwise upon arrival.

Remember how the town's official greeter promised the wheelmen that the "homes" and "hearts" of the community would be open to them? Well, that turned out to apply to barns and jail cells as well:

Some of their number were accommodated by farmers while four slept in the county jail through the kindness of officials.

Remnants of Disaster, 1933

The morning of April 19, 1933 was a sad one on the beaches of Delaware. The waves that day carried in remnants of a national tragedy that is now mostly forgotten.

Coast guardsmen at Cape Henlopen came upon a six-foot-long piece of a catwalk. They found a tabletop and a window, too. The window, marked "Starboard, No. 13," still had glass in it. Nearby in Lewes, guardsmen found the tattered remains of a small mattress or large pillow.

While walking the sand at Bethany Beach, a man named William P. Short found a window frame, a door frame, and a piece of fabric. He said some other folks saw dead bodies floating in the distant sea. If there really were bodies out there, they washed up somewhere else.

When Airships Had Their Moment

The wreckage was from a humongous helium-powered Navy airship, the *Akron*. Built in 1931, she still ranks among the largest flying machines ever made. At 785 feet, she was three times longer than a modern Boeing 747.

Airships were a big deal in the early 1930s. You might

think of them as dirigibles or blimps, but airship was the most popular term. Our military leaders had big plans for these vehicles. They wanted to use them to transport troops. They thought airships would be able to track enemy ships from above. Airships would serve as "aircraft carriers," too, holding up to five small planes that could then launch and land while in midair. It worked like a fledgling version of shuttles coming in and out of the *Starship Enterprise*. Planes were suspended from trapeze-like swing mechanisms that could drop down from the airship's hull.

The *Akron* made her much-ballyhooed "maiden voyage" on Nov. 2, 1931. She cruised down the Eastern seaboard with 207 people on board, proving that she could deliver hundreds of troops at double the speed of a Navy ship and with the freedom to move as the crow flies instead of being limited to navigable waterways. After that the *Akron* logged many hundreds of hours in the air, passing one test after another. She tracked ships off of Cuba. She made it through a 46-hour-long "endurance flight." She participated in a rescue effort around a shipwreck.

Every new flight generated headlines in newspapers around the country. The media treated this airship the way papers treated space shuttle launches in the 1980s, or even the rich-guy rocket launches of more recent vintage. Everyone back then was excited about airships, and for good reason. Here is the historian Richard K. Smith:

[Considering] the rudimentary character of aerial navigation at that date, the Akron's *performance was remarkable. There was not a military airplane in the world in 1932 which could have given the same performance.*

The Crash of 1933
Then came April 3, 1933. The *Akron* was flying the Atlantic

coastline that night, assisting with the calibration of radio signals from various stations and locations. Some navy bigwigs were on board, including a rear admiral. A VP from Mack Trucks was there, too—he was looking at possible ways airships like the *Akron* could be put to use delivering goods in the civilian world.

The *Akron* ran into dense fog off the coast of New Jersey, near Barnegat Bay Lighthouse, which is about halfway between Asbury Park on the north and Atlantic City on the south. The historian Richard Smith again:

Unknown to the men on board ..., they were flying ahead of one of the most violent storm fronts to sweep the North Atlantic States in ten years. It would soon envelop them.

Lightning, rain, wind—it all ramped up into a frenzy. Shortly after midnight, the *Akron's* pilot maneuvered the ship into a rapid descent, but he had trouble stopping that slide. The crew dumped ballast. The ship stabilized at an altitude of just 700 feet. (Remember, the *Akron* was 785 feet long.)

She got back up to a seemingly safe 1,600 feet, but then everything went to hell. The *Akron* dropped into a free-fall, tail-first, at 14 feet per second. When that tail, or "fin," hit the surface, water got inside. That dragged the stern under. Soon enough, the whole airship was breaking into pieces.

Here is an unfathomable thing: The *Akron* had no lifejackets aboard. Not because they weren't invented yet, but because it seems that no one thought about it. There was one rubber life raft, but there wasn't enough time to use it before the *Akron* broke apart. Of the 76 men on board, 73 died. Most deaths were caused by drowning or hypothermia, not crash-related injuries.

Experts believe the accident was caused by one of two things. Pilot error is the most popular theory. Another possibility is that the pilot was relying on readings from a barometric altimeter that had not been properly calibrated.

Either way, the accident wasn't the fault of the airship. But that didn't stop the chorus of doubts and concerns that soon arose over the navy's airship technology. The *Akron* had a sister ship called the *USS Macon*, which continued to pass test after test ... until she ran into a storm off the coast of California in February 1935. A sudden wind shear tore through the gizmos connecting her tailfin to her body. She broke up over the Pacific.

There were 76 men aboard. They were all wearing life jackets. Only two of them died. That second accident was the last straw—the navy soon closed up its airship program and moved on to other projects.

Postscript: An Airship Comeback?

Have you read Phillip Pullman's fantasy trilogy known as *His Dark Materials*? Its two young heroes, Lyra Belacqua and Will Parry, wander through a series of parallel universes while chasing the mysteries of an elementary particle called "Dust." The books are a fun read—and one reason for that is the way they serve up an alternative future in which airships become the primary mode of air transportation.

Some people still think airships will find a role in the future in our universe. A British company, Airlander, is building a new generation of airships in hopes that they can compete in both cargo transportation and passenger travel. One selling point is the fact that airships emit far less carbon dioxide than airplanes. A number of other companies are playing around with airships as well. Lockheed Martin's vessel is aimed at delivering supplies and equipment to disaster zones. Both the Israeli firm Atlas LTA and the French firm Flying Whales have their eye on the shipping-cargo market.

You Wouldn't Believe!

You Wouldn't Believe!

About Secrets of the Eastern Shore

Thank you so much for spending time with this book! The husband-and-wife duo of writer Jim Duffy and photographer Jill Jasuta created Secrets of the Eastern Shore to celebrate the joys and heritage of the Delmarva Peninsula in words, pictures, and products. Their pair has lived near the Choptank River in Cambridge, Md. since 2004.

Duffy started out in newspaper writing in his hometown of Chicago, then got into magazines and books after moving east. Jasuta started in newspapers, too, before transitioning into graphic design and photography.

Both have won numerous awards yada yada yada. ...

Jasuta collects cats. She has recently decided that she loves spiders, too. She's even named a couple of them. Halloween is her favorite holiday.

Much to his own surprise, Duffy fell in love with yoga as an old man. He puts up as best he can with Jill's love of spiders. He prays nightly that his wife never learns to love mosquitoes.

You can always see what these two are up to on the Secrets of the Eastern Shore website. Come join the fun:
SecretsoftheEasternShore.com
Facebook.com/SecretsoftheEasternShore

Other Secrets of the Eastern Shore Books:
• *Eastern Shore Road Trips:*
27 One-Day Adventures on Delmarva
• *Tubman Travels:*
32 Underground Railroad Journeys on Delmarva
• *Eastern Shore Road Trips #2:*
26 MORE One-Day Adventures on Delmarva

You Wouldn't Believe!

The Team

Jim Duffy wrote this book. Any and all errors belong to him and no one else.

Jill Jasuta designed the cover. Check out her latest work here:
• Facebook.com/JillJasutaPhotography
• Instagram.com/JillJasutaPhotography
• SecretsoftheEasternShore.com/product-category/print

Makena Duffy proofread the manuscript and provided research assistance. She is a photographer, artist, and talented wordsmith who lives in New York City.

Paul Clipper designed the interior pages. He is an amateur luthier, award-winning journalist, photographer, graphic artist, and has written several books about the art and adventure of dirt-bike riding. Search his author name at Amazon books for more info.

Special thanks, too, to everyone in the **Secrets of the Eastern Shore community** on Facebook and the website for all the insights, corrections, questions, and encouragement delivered over the years. We have learned so much from you all!

Special kudos and thanks go to **Mary Romanic**, who replied to my cry for help with the title of this book by suggesting *You Wouldn't Believe!*

Thanks again for spending a little time with our work. Here's hoping this book brings a little extra joy into your Delmarva wanderings.

Made in the USA
Middletown, DE
05 September 2024

59779125R00167